Food for the Settler

Bobbie Kalman

The Early Settler Life Series

Toronto
New York

Crabtree Publishing Company

To my sister, Suzie, gourmet cook extraordinaire, with much love

A very special thanks to the following people without whose help this book would not have been possible:

My excellent editorial and art staff: *Lise Gunby, Nancy Cook, Rosemary McLernon, and Nora Peat.*

The skilled photographers who are responsible for the faithful reproductions of historical materials: *Sarah Peters and Stephen Mangione.*

The historians and librarians who provided me with research and photographic opportunities: *William Loos, Margaret Crawford Maloney, Dana Tenny, and Jill Shefrin.* I especially want to thank *Christine Castle and Margaret Perkins of Gibson House, and Nan Wronski of Colborne Lodge for allowing us such unlimited access for our simulations; Bev Hykel of Montgomery's Inn for information and recipes.*

My cooperative and patient models: *Margaret Perkins, Samantha Crabtree, Andrea Crabtree, Peter Crabtree, Lise Gunby, and Kathleen Scherf.*

Cataloging in Publication Data

Kalman, Bobbie.
    Food for the Settler

(Early settler life series)
Includes index.
ISBN   0-86505-013-9 hardcover
ISBN   0-86505-012-0 softcover

1. Food - History.   2. Frontier and pioneer life.   I. Title.   II. Series.

TX19.K35   641'.09'03

350 Fifth Ave, Suite 3308
New York, NY 10118

120 Carlton Street, Suite 309
Toronto, Ontario M5A 4K2

73 Lime Walk
Headington, Oxford OX3 7AD
United Kingdom

Contents

4 From the settler's table to yours
Introduction

5 Everything nature had to offer
*Nature provides the settler with many
sources of food*

6 Fishing the clumsy way

10 Hunting big game

12 Trapping for food

14 Bear with us!
A grizzly tale

16 Birds of a feather
Edible wild birds such as the turkey

18 Wild fruits and berries

20 Preserving the berries

22 Sugar from the bush
The settlers tap the maple-sugar trees

26 How the Indians helped
*The Indians pass on their knowledge of
the natural environment*

30 The vegetable garden
*A good crop means the settlers will
survive*

32 Domestic animals

33 Egg recipes

34 Finger-lickin' chicken

36 Potluck dinners
An entire meal in one pot

38 Bread made with a loving touch
A step-by-step picture story

43 Interesting ways to use bread
*Welsh rabbit, milk toast, flapjacks,
bread pudding, hard sauce, and
pumpkin marmalade*

44 Making butter the old-fashioned way

47 Enough cheese to please
How cheese is made

48 Workday meals
From breakfast through supper

50 Hearty food for hard workers
Working bees end with feasts

52 The apple harvest

56 The fireplace
*The dangers of the fireplace
Hooks, cranes, trammels, and trivets*

58 Brick oven bread-baking

60 Stoves for simpler cooking

61 Kitchens of the future

62 Gadgets galore
Helpful utensils make a cook's job easier

64 Keeping food from spoiling
*Drying, pickling, smoking, potting,
preserving, root cellars, springhouses,
and ice houses*

68 Buying food

70 Selling through advertising
Packaged goods appear on the shelves

72 Food for thought
The science of homemaking

74 No speaking, smelling, spitting, spilling,
or smacking
Table manners for settlers

76 Tea party recipes
Dainty snacks for special occasions

78 Cold, sweet, and sticky
Children enjoy making ice cream

80 Taffy for a pulling party
*Taffy pulling is a good excuse for a
get-together*

82 Dishes brought from different lands

84 The Thanksgiving feast
*The settlers celebrate a successful
harvest*

86 Christmas dinner, the biggest meal of
the year
Delicious dishes for Christmas

88 The glorious plum pudding parade
The old symbol of Christmas

92 The Christmas birds
Recipes for turkey and goose

94 The blessing of food
The settlers give thanks

95 Glossary   Index

We are almost ready to embark on our food trek. First, we pause to wash our hands.

We will take you on a taste adventure such as you have never enjoyed before. As an example, what could delight the taste buds more than hot homemade bread straight from the oven?

From the settler's table to yours

Food for the Settler is a food odyssey. We begin our travels with the first pioneers in the bush. We have to search for our food. Dinner is wild berries and squirrel pie. We also eat venison, moose, and bear. We catch our fish in frying pans. The Indians show us how to tap trees for our sugar.

We soon settle into a life of farming. We grow our own crops and raise our own animals. Our food world is made up of potluck dinners and homemade bread and butter.

The next phase of our journey takes place in the settler's world of plenty. We enjoy not just plain suppers, but sumptuous feasts. We are able to buy some of our food. Someone has even put food into cans for us. We cook on a stove instead of a fireplace. Our Thanksgiving and Christmas dinners are so big that we fear the table will break under their weight.

Our food journey allows us to sample food at each stage of our travels. We can try

the same foods the settlers used to eat. All the recipes presented here are from old cookbooks, magazines or settler diaries. They have been tested and have been changed in some cases to suit our kitchens. The recipes in *italics* are originals and have not been changed. These are either easy enough to use from the original, or are not suitable for our purposes. For example, roasting a haunch of venison might be too much of a challenge for a modern kitchen. We have a small suggestion. If you want to try these recipes and are on the young side, why not ask for some adult help?

Besides trying recipes, we explore a pioneer kitchen, learn to make bread and butter the old-fashioned way, and learn about the table manners of our hosts.

Our journey through food is an exciting adventure of sight, taste, and smell. We end our odyssey giving thanks for our blessings, of which food is a very great part.

The early settlers did not have to worry about food. The forests, skies, lakes, and streams offered plenty to eat. However, not all the settlers knew how to hunt or fish as well as these two pioneers.

Everything nature had to offer

The early pioneers brought only a few supplies with them. As soon as they reached their destination they had to find more food. They were lucky because the woods were filled with animals, plants, birds, and berries. The seas, lakes, rivers, and streams teemed with fish. The early settlers could hunt, trap, fish, and gather berries and other fruit to stay alive. The native people taught them how to plant crops that would grow well in the new land. If a family of settlers worked hard, they could build a house, clear some land, and plant crops in just a few weeks' time. The next year, the extra crops could be put away or bartered for animals, such as chickens, geese, pigs, sheep, and cows. The more crops and vegetables a settler could grow, the more could be traded for other goods.

The settlers did not know how to fish at first. This shark is bigger than any fish they have ever seen. If they cannot hook it, they will beat it with a club. They might even have to shoot it.

Fishing the clumsy way

If the early settlers could choose where to live, they picked land that was near water. Water was needed for drinking, cooking, and washing. Water also meant plenty of fish for dinner. The only problem was that the early settlers were not very good at catching them! Some of the settlers tried to catch fish with frying pans. Others brought horses into the rivers to step on the fish. Flour sifters were sometimes used to scoop up the fish. The Indians showed the settlers how to tread out eels from the brook with their feet and catch them with their hands. Beating fish with sticks was another clumsy way the settlers tried to stop the slippery slickers.

Those who lived near the sea could easily dig for clams, catch crabs, or spear lobsters. There were oceans of oysters which could be eaten raw or made into delicious stews. The settlers soon realized what treasures the waters held. As the new ships came from Europe, they carried fishing nets, hooks, and lines. The settlers learned how to make their own fishing tackle. Fish soon became a large part of the country's export trade to Europe

Broiled fish

There were many delicious ways to cook fish. The settlers found the Indian way of broiling fish simple and tasty. You

Bob, Joe, and Tom hope to catch at least ten fish today. They promised their mother that they would bring back enough for fish soup. The fallen tree makes a perfect seat over the water.

might try it on your barbecue at home. Cover your fish with foil first. Here is the way the Indians taught the settlers to do it.

"Take a fish fresh out of the water. Cut out the entrails and without removing the scales, wash it clean. Dry it in a cloth or in the grass and cover it all over with clear hot ashes. When the flesh will part from the bone, draw the fish from the ashes, strip off the skin, and it is fit for the table."

Small fish caught by small fry

In the spring the lakes, rivers, and brooks were filled with fish that children could catch easily. These smaller fish, such as perch, sunfish, and trout, tasted best when made into a hearty soup. The ingredients in the recipe below are not exact, so taste as you cook and add spices as desired.

Catch-of-the-day soup

"After cleaning, boil the smallest fish of the catch in a big pot of water. When the fish have broken into pieces, strain them through a colander into a stewing pan. Season with pepper, salt, parsley, savory, and thyme. Add a few chopped chives and a young onion. Clean and scale some of the larger fish in the catch. Cut these into your soup. Mix 5 mL of fine flour, a slice of butter, and 15 mL of tomato catsup. Add these ingredients to 250 mL of milk. When the soup boils, stir this mixture in and remove the pot from the fire. Your soup is ready to eat."

Those who had no fishing poles or nets could still spear a dinner from the sea.

Fishing was a good source of food even in winter. The settlers learned to catch fish through the ice.

The salmon run

It was easy to spear salmon as they traveled upstream from the sea and lakes. There were so many that they filled the rivers. When the settlers wanted to catch the salmon for dinner, they cut down a tree and put it across the river. They stood on the log and speared the salmon when they swam by. Here is an old recipe for salmon that you can make in the modern way.

Salmon croquettes

200 mL	salmon
1	egg, well beaten
120 mL	fine bread crumbs
15 mL	butter
	flour, enough to coat croquettes
	salt to taste
	cayenne pepper to taste
	dash of nutmeg
	juice of ½ lemon
	parsley to garnish

Drain the liquid from the salmon and set aside. Mash the fish with a fork until it is broken into little pieces. Melt butter and pour over salmon. Add salt, pepper, nutmeg, and lemon juice. If the mixture is too dry, pour in a bit of the salmon liquid. Add the crumbs and mix with a spoon or clean hands. Divide the mixture into separate croquettes. It is up to you to make the croquettes as big or as small as you want them. Flour the croquettes and set in a cold place for an hour. Fry the croquettes in hot oil and serve on a warm platter. Garnish with fresh parsley.

White sauce for fish

Salmon croquettes, or all fish for that matter, taste even better with a white sauce poured on top.

250 mL	cream
60 mL	butter
10 mL	flour
	salt and pepper to taste
	sprinkle of parsley
5 mL	lemon juice

Melt the butter in a saucepan. Add the flour, salt and pepper, parsley, and lemon juice. Slowly add cream and heat, stirring until mixture thickens. Do not boil. Pour over fish.

These people decided to cook the clams they found into a chowder right on the beach. The boy in front does not find the chowder to his taste. Try the recipe below and see what you think of it.

Clam chowder for a beach party

Those who lived near the sea often cooked their clam chowder on the beach. If you cannot find a beach, try this chowder recipe in your kitchen.

60 mL	chopped salt pork or bacon
120 mL	minced onion
2	medium potatoes
400 mL	canned clams, with juice
15 mL	lemon juice
500 mL	milk
	pepper to taste
	nutmeg to taste

In a large saucepan, fry bacon and onion until bacon is crisp and onion tender. Stir in milk. Heat gently, stirring occasionally. Stir in clams with juice, lemon juice, and a sprinkling of pepper and nutmeg. Heat through.

Melissa wonders whether catching this crab was worth it. The pain in her finger has brought tears to her eyes.

Skinning a moose is a big job for many hands. Ralph rolls up his sleeve, ready to tackle his end of the work.

These hunters have shot enough food for at least a week. Besides the deer, they are also bringing home a rabbit and a couple of birds.

Hunting big game

Just as the waters were filled with fish, the woods were filled with birds and animals. Instead of buying their meat, the early settlers had to hunt their own. There were many moose, deer and elk in the forest. Bringing one of these large animals home meant not having to hunt for a while. Venison, or deer meat, was therefore a welcome treat for the settler family. One settler tells us how she prepared venison.

Venison roast

"The best joints to roast are the haunch and the loins. If the deer is fat and in good season, the meat needs no other basting than the fat which runs from it. But the meat is often lean, so it is often necessary to use lard, butter, or slices of bacon fat to assist the roasting. Venison should be cooked over a brisk fire, basted often, and a little salt thrown over it."

Venison was cooked over the fire in the fireplace. A basting pan caught the drippings from the meat and fat. These drippings were poured over the meat to keep it from becoming dry. Venison was also fried, put into pies, or eaten after it was smoked. As venison could be dry, the settlers often made a gravy to serve with it.

Venison gravy

"A little seasoning of onion may be added to the drippings. A dusting of flour put in the pan with a bit of boiling water and a little tomato catsup will make the gravy."

There he is, behind the rock!

Catch his hoof, Ted! Catch his hoof!

Trapping for food

If the settlers were not able to hunt big game, they had to trap smaller animals such as beavers, rabbits, raccoons, squirrels, and even skunks. Old cookbooks contain recipes for squirrel pies, raccoon stew, and beaver-tail steaks. The thought of eating any of these animals is not very appealing to us today. However, when the settlers were hungry, they had to eat whatever they could catch.

"When we found it impossible to get any meat, the different kinds of squirrels supplied us with pies, stews, and roasts. Our barn stood at the top of the hill near the bush. In a trap set for such 'small deer' (the name we called the squirrels), we often caught from ten to twelve a day."

Bear meat was good to eat

The backwoods settlers were often visited by bears. Bears came to steal food from

Bringing in that bear sure was hard work. I think I'll rest for a while.

the settlers but sometimes a bear ended up as the settlers' dinner. One settler told how she had to shoot a bear that had broken into her storage shed. She did not like the idea of eating bear meat, so she kept one of the bear's legs and fed the rest of the meat to the dogs. After roasting the leg, she was sorry she did not keep all of the meat because it was so tender and full of flavor.

A bear trap.

Easy now! He's a big one!

Bear with us!

One way or another the settlers discovered that bear meat was good to eat. Can you bear the idea of biting into a bear bone? I find it unbearable! And so did the bears! How could the settlers then expect the bears to grin and bear the situation? Of course the bears had to bare their teeth in anger. Did the settlers expect the bears to eat only berries?

No wonder the bears fought back! So settlers had to bear witness to many bear break-ins. Doors were no barriers for bears. No barricade could keep out a big bear. Because bears did not usually bear good tidings, the settlers found it hard to bear up with bare hands. So the settlers had to bear arms against the bears. Some-times the bears chased the settlers deep into the forest. The settlers were in danger of losing their bearings! Bears also chased the settlers up trees. Some settlers barely escaped! And these are just the bare bones of the settler and bear battles. Oh, what grizzly days those must have been!

This settler is happy that he was able to find such a big turkey for his Christmas meal. Now his family will have enough meat to last until the New Year.

Grandfather weighs the turkey Dad brought in. The whole family works hard to prepare a wonderful dinner.

Birds of a feather

Wild birds provided food for the pioneers. Ducks, geese, pheasants, quail, partridge, and grouse all tasted delicious in soups, stews, pies, and roasts. Passenger pigeons were so numerous that they could be caught in nets. Some boys used another method to catch the pigeons. They tied the pigeons they had trapped onto poles. Other pigeons would soon join the tied pigeons and become the boys' shooting targets. So many passenger pigeons were shot that they are extinct today.

Tricking turkeys

The settlers discovered that wild turkeys were very good food. Turkeys soon became part of every big holiday meal. Some of the wild turkeys weighed as much as 20 kg. Turkeys could be shot or bagged. Some hunters learned to imitate the mating call of the turkey. When the turkey came close

enough to the hunter, a bag was thrown over its head. Some settlers went turkey hunting by moonlight. Others built turkey pens. A trail of corn was sprinkled outside the pen. The trail led to the hole through which the turkey entered the pen. When the corn was eaten the turkeys raised their heads and could no longer see the entrance hole. They were trapped.

In later days the settlers domesticated the wild turkey. The domesticated turkey was more moist than the wild turkey. However, many settlers still preferred the taste of the wild turkey.

Blackberry time

Now the glorious sunshine of summer is
   past,
And the crisp leaves of autumn are
   reddening fast,
Full well does each rosy-cheeked country
   child know,
That the season is come when the blackberries grow.

Then bring out the baskets; we'll wander
   away
'Mid the thick tangled hedges throughout
   the long day;
Till with evening returning we'll sing as
   we go,
Down the dark wooded lanes where the
   blackberries grow.

Wild fruits and berries

The settlers could not live by meat alone! They needed the vitamins and fiber that fruit and vegetables provided. While the settlers waited for their crops to be ready for harvesting, they collected all kinds of berries which grew wild in the woods. There were blackberries, gooseberries, cranberries and blueberries. Wild currants, both black and red, were found in swampy areas, along with wild plums and choke-cherries.

On the open plains the settlers found huckleberries and delicious sweet straw-berries. Raspberries were good for eating and for making into drinks.

"A dish of raspberries and milk with sugar, or raspberries in a pie, gives many an emigrant family a supper. The black rasp-berry makes the best pie, and this fruit dries better than the red, as it is sweeter and richer in quality."

Raspberry quencher was a cool drink for hot summer days. Both children and adults enjoyed it. Raspberry tea, made from the dried leaves of the raspberry bush, was a good substitute for tea and coffee. Delicious drinks could be made from any of the berries found in the woods and fields. The recipe below can also be made with blue-berries, blackberries, currants, or straw-berries. The recipe has been adapted from the original.

Would you like another glass of raspberry quencher?

Raspberry quencher

Mix 1 L of white vinegar with 2 L of raspberries. Let the mix stand for 24 hours. Drain the liquid through a sieve. Add 2 L of raspberries to the strained liquid and let stand. The next day strain and add 2 L more of berries. Put the liquid into the top of a double boiler. Add 250 mL sugar for every 500 mL of liquid. (Measure the liquid as you put it into the pot.) Stir the sugar into the raspberry liquid until melted. Store the syrup in bottles for two weeks to allow the flavor to develop.

When you need a refreshing drink, just add a small amount (30–50 mL) to a glass of plain or soda water, or make the quencher up in a pitcher.

This is not the way to make cherry jam!

Preserving the berries

The settlers preserved much of their fruit. First they boiled it with a little sugar until it was thick. Then they spread the fruit on sheets of paper to dry in the sun. The papers were rolled up and hung in a dry place. If a settler wanted to make blueberry pie in the middle of winter, all she had to do was take some dried blueberries from the paper rolls and boil them in water with sugar. The blueberries looked and tasted almost as good as the fresh ones did.

Blueberry pie

You too can enjoy blueberry pie any time. If you cannot find fresh blueberries, use frozen ones.

Pie Crust

500 mL	flour
5 mL	salt
165 mL	lard
70 mL	cold water

Put flour and salt into a bowl. Cut in half of the lard until finely mixed. Cut in the other half until the dough forms lumps the size of peas. Sprinkle in the water about 15 mL at a time. Mix gently as you sprinkle in the water, until the dough comes almost free from the sides of the bowl. Press into a ball. Let rest for a few minutes and then cut in half and roll on a floured cloth.

Blueberry filling

1 L	blueberries
120 mL	sugar
85 mL	flour
15 mL	butter

Preheat oven to 220° C. Mix ingredients and spoon into an unbaked pie shell. Cover with top pastry and slit holes for steam to escape. Bake until crust is golden brown and berries are bubbling, about 50 minutes.

Strawberry jam

Berries that were not dried were usually preserved as jams. The settlers made their jams with much more sugar than we would today. We have adapted an old recipe and used less sugar. The recipe for strawberry jam can also be used to make raspberry, blueberry, cherry, and currant jam.

1 L	strawberries
300 mL	sugar

Wash strawberries and remove hulls. Cut into slices. Sprinkle a thin layer of sugar on the bottom of a large, heavy pot. Add a layer of strawberry slices, another layer of sugar, and so on, until you have used up all the fruit and sugar. Make sure the top layer of strawberries is covered with sugar. Let stand 4 to 5 hours.

Wash your jam jars inside and out. Sterilize them by boiling them in a large pot of water for 15-20 minutes. The jars should still be hot when you are ready to fill them. Sterilize the lids as well. Sterilization will kill the bacteria which could spoil your jam. It is your most important step.

Put your fruit and sugar on high heat and boil. Reduce to low heat and cook, stirring often, for 45-60 minutes. Use a candy thermometer to test your jam. When it reaches the temperature of 110° C, it is ready. Ladle the jam into jars and seal immediately.

Fresh blueberry pie, ready for the oven.

In the top part of the picture the sap is being brought in for boiling. The women, left, are making sugar from part of the syrup. Middle left, two pioneers cut holes for spiles. Center, a boy chops wood to keep the fire hot. Lower right, a father shows his son how to empty a trough filled with sap into the bucket.

One man stands by watching the sap boil as the others take a break from their sweet, but tiring, work.

Sugar from the bush

White sugar was made from sugar cane which grew in the south. The early settlers were not able to get enough white sugar for all their needs. One could buy white sugar at the general store, but it was expensive. The settlers used it only for special occasions. There was another type of sugar which the bush offered in great abundance. It was maple sugar. At first the settlers did not know about this type of sugar. The Indians taught the settlers how to tap the sugar maple trees to get sap. The sap was boiled down into syrup and sugar.

The sap starts to flow

On about March 20 when the days became warm and the nights were still cold, the sap started to run in the trees. The first sap tapped made the best sugar. The later sap was made into molasses. The first thing the settlers did before they tapped any of the trees was clear the underbrush

and rotten logs from around the maple trees. Next they chose the boiling place. It was in the center of the sugar bush, not too far from any of the trees. A shelter or shanty was built for the *sugaring-off*. Roads were cut in many directions to allow the ox-carts or sleds to get through.

Each sugar maple tree was tapped with a small auger. Hollow round tubes, or *spiles*, were driven into the holes about 3 cm deep. The sap ran out into troughs made from trunks of pine, black ash, cherry, or butternut trees. From these troughs the sap was poured into buckets, barrels, and then into the kettles in which the sap was boiled down into syrup. Milk or eggs were added to the syrup while it was boiling. The dirt, insects, and pieces of bark in the syrup rose to the top and were trapped in the milk or egg foam. The foam was skimmed off the top of the syrup along with the impurities.

No one wants to miss the best part of making maple syrup, the sugaring-off process. Children watch wide-eyed as the syrup hardens into sugar. The woman, left, is pulling some taffy that has been made with the syrup. On the right, Melinda Strickland is making her delicious "maple sweeties."

Sugaring-off

Children looked forward to *sugaring-off*. As described by a young settler, it was a sweet experience.

"We boiled down a small amount of sap to the thickness of heavy syrup, which we dropped with wooden spoons upon hard snow. It cooled almost immediately, and was so crispy and sweet that we ate it until we really could eat no more."

Maple sap was also made into molasses, maple vinegar, maple beer, and maple wine.

Along with syrup, candy, and molasses, the settlers came away from the sugar bush with funny stories. One settler and his nephew were boiling syrup for the first time. They were not sure how thick the syrup should be, so they kept pouring it into the snow. They tasted and tested until all the syrup had disappeared into their stomachs.

The sweet bull

Not only people liked the sweet syrup. Cows, bulls, and dogs were also crazy about it. One bull had to learn the hard way that maple sugar could be dangerous to his health.

"We were alarmed by a loud bellow, and on looking in the direction of the boilers, were horrified at seeing our bull, Prince, running off with his tail in the air, and followed, in his mad rush, by several other head of cattle. I knew something was the matter, and, on hurrying to the boilers, I found the rascally bull had popped his head into one of my tins of hot sugar. The heat of the syrup had so shocked his nerves that he made off with the best part of the liquid sticking round his muzzle."

Another time three cows, owned by the same settler, drank so much molasses that the settler had to pump their stomachs. This unfortunate person finally found a way to keep his cows and bulls

David goes for more sap as his mother keeps warm and watches the syrup cooking. This photograph was taken in a sugar bush in 1865.

out of the syrup. However, he never could figure out how to keep the two-footed predators away.

Two-footed predators

"Besides trouble arising from four-footed creatures, you are apt to receive many visits from young ladies and children, who, somehow or another, never make their appearance during the first part of the operation when there is work to do. They wait patiently until the syrup is ready for testing. Then spoons, tins, and ladles are in great demand for tasting purposes."

Maple sweeties

One settler had a great many visitors because his sister's maple sugar "sweeties" were so delicious that they were famous throughout the area. This is how she described making them.

"When sugaring-off, take a little of the thickest syrup into a saucer, stir in a very little fine flour and a small bit of butter, and flavor with essence of lemon, peppermint, or ginger, as you like best. When cold, cut into little bricks about 3 cm in length. This makes a cheap treat for the little ones. By melting down a piece of maple sugar and adding a bit of butter and flavoring, you can always give children sweeties, if you think it proper to allow them treats of this sort."

A sweet taste for meat

Maple syrup was not only eaten as a sweet. It was used as an ingredient in many dishes, such as Johnny Cake and Beans with Pork. The Indians used to dip their meat into the syrup for flavor. Since then, we too have discovered that it makes roast ham, pork, or chicken taste delicious. Try your next roast of meat with a coating of maple syrup.

INDIAN VEGETABLE FOOD RESOURCES

Camass Flowers

Digging Camass roots used for food by Western Indians.

Collecting Maple Sap

Service Berries

Eaten fresh, or dried & mixed with buffalo meat to make pemmican.

The settlers learned about maple syrup from the Indians. The Indians also taught the settlers how to use berries and roots as part of their food.

The settlers bartered with huge iron pots to get furs and meat. The Indians found the pots especially useful for boiling down maple sap.

The most important lesson the Indians taught the settlers was how to grow corn.

How the Indians helped

The Indians taught the settlers to hunt, trap, and use the resources the forest offered. The Indian children taught the settler children which wild plants were safe to eat. Together the children searched for mushrooms, onions, celery, dandelion greens, and wild leeks. They hunted for all kinds of berries and nuts. All of this food kept the settlers from going hungry.

The most important lesson the Indian taught the settler was how to grow corn. Corn was a very important food for the new settlers. It grew in almost any kind of soil. It could be eaten in many ways. The settlers made bread, cake, cereal, and pudding with it. The Indians showed the settlers how to roast corn on the cob over an open fire. They taught the settlers the magic of popping corn.

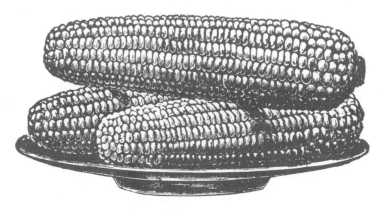

Husking corn is hard work, but these boys do not mind. Tonight they will be able to roast some of it on an open fire.

Grown together, eaten together

Clearing land for crops was a difficult job. The trees had to be cut down and the logs burned. The settlers needed to get as much use as possible out of the land they cleared. After the corn was in, the settlers could plant beans and squash between the rows of corn. This method of planting made it possible to grow many vegetables in a small area of land. The Indians taught the settlers how to cook, as well as grow, these vegetables together. This vegetable mixture was called *succotash*. An early settler recipe we found for corn stew must have come from an Indian succotash recipe. The settlers added meat to the vegetables. We have made the recipe easier so that you can try it.

Corn stew

750 mL	corn (canned or frozen)
3	slices of bacon
3	chicken breasts
5	green onions
250 mL	carrots
120 mL	lima beans
2	large tomatoes
2	stalks celery
1	green pepper
250 mL	chicken stock
	salt to taste
	pepper to taste

Chop the bacon and fry in a deep frying pan until almost crisp. Add chopped onions. Take the meat off the chicken breasts and cut into small pieces. Add to bacon and onions. Put the chicken bones into 500 mL water and boil for 20 minutes. Brown the chicken meat with the bacon and onions. Chop celery, green pepper,

WILD RICE

EAR OF WILD RICE

HARVESTING

Wild rice was an important cereal food among the Indians of the Great Lakes region.

DRYING

HULLING

WINNOWING

The Indians grew their own rice, which they bartered or sold to the settlers. Indian rice grew in lakes with muddy bottoms. Today we call this rice "wild rice." You can find some at your grocery store.

carrots and tomatoes. Brown these vegetables in the bacon fat together with the chicken and onions. Add the corn and stir. Your chicken stock should be ready by now. Pour 250 mL of it over your mixture and simmer stew for 30 minutes. You can eat your stew from a bowl with a piece of Johnny Cake, or if you prefer, serve it over wild rice.

Johnny cake

If you are serving your stew with Johnny Cake, you will need the recipe. Johnny Cake is a little like bread. The settlers learned to make it from the Indians. The settlers loved it because it was simple and quick to prepare. There is very little one can do to ruin it. Why don't you try this recipe and invite your friends over to share the cake with you. It is good plain, with soup or stew, with butter, or with jam or marmalade.

250 mL	cornmeal
250 mL	flour (any kind)
60 mL	melted butter
1	egg
60 mL	brown sugar (or white if you like)
60 mL	molasses
250 mL	milk
20 mL	baking soda
5 mL	ginger
5 mL	salt

Preheat oven to 220° C. Mix ingredients and pour into greased square cake pan. Bake 20–30 minutes. The cake is done when a knife stuck in the center comes out clean.

The vegetable garden

The settlers had to grow as many crops as they could as quickly as possible. A good harvest meant having food. A better harvest meant having goods to barter with. The settlers could sell their extra crops and buy animals or tools for farming.

Planting crops was even more important than making the settlers' homes comfortable. The settlers knew that if they were to stay in the new land, they had to become self-sufficient quickly. They could not hope to live off the wilderness forever. Soon other settlers would come and the wilderness would turn into a village or a town. Growing food would become the livelihood of many people.

The settlers took pride in the crops they grew. No other accomplishment was more important to them. One settler wrote in her diary:

"We had at first no chairs to sit upon, only nail-kegs and packing-cases, but we had a garden. And such a garden! There were rows upon rows of peas, lima beans, sweet corn, sweet potatoes, squashes, pumpkins, and melons - both scented and watermelons."

A good crop was the first sign of success for the new settlers. It meant that they could survive in their new home. They put their energy and sweat into the land and the land rewarded them with food.

Enough onions to make me cry!

Pumpkins were used in the same ways as apples. They were baked in pies, dried in pieces, or made into marmalade.

Vegetable recipes for you to try

Stuffed tomatoes

Use big, firm tomatoes. Cut a thin slice from the bottom opposite the stem. Carefully take out the seeds and juice without breaking the tomatoes. Mix the seeds and juice with stale bread crumbs, salt, pepper, a bit of chopped onion, chopped ham, and enough butter to moisten the mixture. Stuff the tomatoes and put them into a baking dish. Sprinkle them with a little of the mixture and a topping of plain, dry crumbs. Bake for at least 30 minutes in a moderate oven, about 175° C.

Hot slaw

Thinly slice a cabbage and sprinkle it with salt and pepper. In a pan heat a mixture of 30 mL butter and 120 mL vinegar. In a third container mix 2 raw eggs, 200 mL cream, and 120 mL sugar. Stir this last mixture into the heated vinegar. Add the cabbage. Heat gently until very tender.

Stewed celery with cream

Cut 6 celery heads into pieces. Boil in salted water until they are tender. Put 250 mL cream and a touch of mace into a pan. Warm the cream until it thickens. When ready to eat, put the celery in bowls and cover with cream. Stewed celery may also be served on toast with butter on top.

Hearty potato soup

Of all the vegetables the settlers grew, potatoes, next to corn, were eaten most often. Potato soup was a filling dish which could be served hot or cold.

3		freshly boiled potatoes
1		boiled onion
15	mL	butter
500	mL	milk
10	mL	flour
		sprinkle of parsley
		dash of salt
		dash of pepper

Pour milk into a medium-sized pot. Throw in onion slices. Heat for 2 minutes, but do not boil. Mash potatoes and add to hot milk. Add a dash of salt and pepper. Put through a wire strainer or mix at a slow speed with electric mixer. In a small pan melt butter and add flour. Stir well. Drop a little milk on this, stirring well, and pour into soup. Let simmer 10 minutes. Add chopped parsley, and a little milk if the soup is too thick. Serve hot or cold.

Paring potatoes for a hearty soup.

Farm animals were raised for eggs, milk and meat.

These geese may be vicious, but they sure taste delicious!

Domestic animals

Raising domestic animals was important to the settlers. Cows provided the settlers with milk, butter, and cheese. Sheep were raised for wool. Without wool, the settlers could not make warm winter clothes. The tallow or fat that came from the sheep was used for making candles. And, of course, sheep provided meat.

Animals had many uses, but their most important purpose was to supply settlers with plenty of food. Pigs were turned into hams, bacon, roasts, and chops. The fat of the pigs was used for frying and baking. It was called *lard*. Geese, chickens, ducks, and guinea fowl also provided an important part of the settlers' diet. Not only was their meat good to eat, but these birds also laid eggs.

Egg recipes

Eggs were used in cakes, puddings, sauces, and sandwiches. One of the first solid foods given to children one hundred years ago was soft custard. Custard is still a favorite dessert today. It is good on its own, with fresh fruit, caramel sauce, or maple syrup. Try this basic recipe and make your own toppings.

Soft custard

250 mL	milk
1	egg
30 mL	sugar
	dash of salt
	pinch of nutmeg

Heat the milk until hot but not boiling. Beat egg and add sugar and salt. Pour the hot milk into the egg mixture, beating well. Pour into the upper part of a double boiler and cook until custard thickens. Pour into custard or pudding cups. Sprinkle with nutmeg and chill. Serve cold.

Picnic surprise

The settlers loved picnics. One of their favorite picnic foods was Stuffed Eggs. Here is the recipe.

Boil 6 eggs for 7-10 minutes. Remove eggs from boiling water and put in cold water. When cool, remove shells and cut each egg lengthwise into halves. Carefully take out the yolks and put into a bowl. Leave the matching egg whites together in pairs. Put into a bowl:

15 mL	melted butter
3 mL	mustard
3 mL	salt
	dash of cayenne pepper

Mash these ingredients into the yolks until you make a paste. Make little yolk-sized balls from the paste. Put each ball into one side of a white of egg, and cover with the other side. Your egg will look whole again, and contain a lovely surprise for your guests to savor. Instead of tasting just plain yolks, your friends will goo and gush over your mildly mustardy mellow mush.

If you count on catching fish for your picnic, you might go hungry.

Lard comes from the fat of pigs. It was used for cooking, baking, and frying.

"Here chick, chick, chick!"

34

Finger-lickin' chicken

And where there were eggs, there were chickens not far behind! Or was it the chickens that came first? In any case, here are two old chicken recipes that are sure to please. The recipes have been changed to suit modern kitchens.

Crispy fried chicken

Almost everyone's favorite way of eating chicken is with the fingers. The best type of finger chicken is fried chicken. It is a favorite now, and it was a favorite then. There are different ways to make it. Try the old-fashioned crispy way.

1	fryer chicken, cut into pieces
60 mL	butter
60 mL	lard
150 mL	flour

A few hours before you are ready to fry your chicken, sprinkle the chicken pieces with salt. Put the pieces into a bowl and cover with cold water. Let stand for about 30 minutes.

Pour the water off the chicken and shake off excess. Roll pieces in flour. Fry the chicken in hot butter and lard. Brown the chicken on both sides for 5 minutes. Cover with tight lid. Continue to fry chicken on lower heat for 30-40 minutes. Remove the lid for the last 5 minutes of cooking to crisp chicken. Enjoy your finger-licking treat!

Roast chicken with stuffing and gravy

Remove giblets from chicken and dry the inside with a paper towel. Stuff chicken with the stuffing, below. Sew or skewer closed the opening. Season with pepper, seasoning salt, and a sprinkle of flour. Roast for about 1½ hours at 175° C. Baste chicken often with its own juices. Serve with gravy.

Stuffing

2	slices bacon, cut up
3	slices white bread
30 mL	butter
1	egg
	handful of finely chopped parsley
	pinch of savory
	pinch of marjoram

Fry bacon until almost crisp. Cut bread into cubes. Add egg, butter, herbs, and bacon with its grease left over from frying. Mix together well with clean hands. Stuff mixture into chicken. (For a more moist stuffing, we suggest adding 120 mL raisins, chopped apples, or apricots.

Everyday gravy

The settlers liked gravy on their meat, as we do. Here is an easy recipe that can be suited to your tastes.

250 mL	water
30 mL	butter
45 mL	flour
	salt to taste
	pan drippings

In a pan heat half of the water with the butter. Mix the other half with the flour until there are no lumps. Add a little of the hot mixture to the cold and pour it all into the pan, stirring constantly. Simmer until the gravy thickens. Add pan drippings. You can give your gravy a personal touch by adding chopped parsley, mushrooms, or onions. Serve gravy with chicken, stuffing, and vegetables of your choice.

The above recipes for stuffing and gravy can also be used for turkey and Cornish hens.

No scrambled eggs today!

Oh, how their hearts will burn after this pot of beans!

Potluck dinners

The settlers did not have many pots and pans. Pots and pans used in fireplace cooking were very expensive and difficult to get. When a settler cooked supper, the whole meal was usually made in one pot. Stews and soups of meat and vegetables were hot, hearty, and filling. There was nothing like a good jack rabbit stew with dumplings, an Irish lamb stew, or everyone's favorite, baked beans with pork.

The pot of baked beans

O! how my heart burns for my new home-
  land,
Where potatoes and squashes and cucumbers
  grow;
Where cheer and good welcome are always
  at hand,
And custards and pumpkin pies smoke in
  a row;
But my heart to another food quite strongly
  leans,
Yes, far dearer to me, is a pot of baked
  beans.

A pot of baked beans! with what pleasure
  I saw it,
Well seasoned, well porked, with my
  mother's light touch;
And when from the glowing hot oven
  she'd draw it,
Well crisped and well browned, how I love
  it so much!
O, give me my supper, the food of my
  dreams,
Some dark Johnny Cake, and a pot of
  baked beans.

Baked beans with pork

You have probably eaten pork and beans from the can many times. Now it is time for you to learn how to make it from scratch. You can make it in a slow-cooker or bake it at a low temperature in your oven.

500 mL	navy beans
	water
7.5 mL	salt
7.5 mL	pepper

200 g	salt pork
650 mL	canned tomatoes
250 mL	diced onions
125 mL	molasses
125 mL	maple syrup
7.5 mL	dry mustard
125 mL	hot water

The night before, rinse beans and cover with about 3 L of water. Let the beans soak overnight.

The next day, put beans on stove and bring to a boil. Add salt. Simmer for 30 minutes or until the skins split. Cut salt pork into small pieces. Place some pieces in the bottom of a crock pot. Mix together molasses, syrup, mustard, seasonings, and hot water. Drain beans and mix with the tomatoes and onions. Place in a crock pot on top of pork. Pour molasses mixture into the beans. Place the rest of the salt pork in the middle of the beans. Make sure there is enough liquid to cover the beans. There should be at least 1 cm more liquid than the beans. Cover with lid and bake 8-10 hours at low heat. Check once in a while to make sure there is enough liquid. Add more water if necessary.

Irish stew

We have inherited this great recipe from the many Irish settlers. It can double as a beef stew as well. Simply substitute beef for lamb. This type of stew could easily be made with any meat. It is a good, basic "dinner in a pot" recipe.

45 mL	vegetable oil
1 kg	lamb shoulder, cut into cubes
2	onions, chopped
500 mL	beef broth
3	medium potatoes, peeled and cut into 8-10 chunks
2	carrots, cut into chunks
5 mL	salt
5 mL	pepper
5 mL	marjoram
2 mL	thyme
	dusting of flour

Cover meat pieces with a dusting of flour. Brown them in hot vegetable oil. Drain off excess fat. Add onions and carrots. Cook and stir for 2-3 minutes or until onion is soft. Pour broth over meat, onions, and carrots. Cover and simmer for 2 hours. Stir in potatoes and seasoning. Cover and simmer for 25 minutes. Skim off fat. Add a little water if the stew is too thick.

Supper in a pan

If the settler's pot was being used for making candles, a whole dinner could also have been cooked in one pan. An old-time pan dinner favorite was called "Bubble and Squeak." Try it! Here is the original 1848 recipe.

Bubble and squeak

"Cut slices from cold beef. Fry them quickly until brown, and put them in a dish to keep hot. Clean the fat from the pan, and put into it greens (use cooked cabbage) and carrots previously boiled and chopped small, and a little butter, pepper, and salt. Make the vegetables and seasonings very hot, and put them around the beef with a little gravy. Cold pork boiled is better material for Bubble and Squeak than beef, which is always hard; in either case these should be very thin and lightly fried."

Bubble and squeak, the one-pan dinner.

Margaret pretended to be our grandmother for the day. With her help we learned to make bread the old-fashioned way. Read the recipe and follow the picture story to find out how we did it. Perhaps you can invite your grandmother to share your bread-making experience with you. Happy loafing!

Mix ingredients thoroughly with a spoon.

Bread made with a loving touch

Making bread the pioneer way is a good way of reaching back into the past. We spent a day exploring the warm, friendly kitchen of Gibson House which was the home of settlers in the 1850s. It took nearly a whole morning to make bread and butter. But what a wonderful time it was! We pretended that Margaret, our guide, was our grandmother. She was patient, helpful, and one of the kindest people we had ever met. It made us feel good to be in her kitchen, just as it must have made the children of the settlers feel happy to be in the presence of their grandmothers. In those days grandparents usually lived in the same home as the grandchildren. The bread we baked that day was made with care and a special kind of love. It was the love that a grandmother of 130 years ago would have shared with her grandchildren as she taught them the art of bread-making.

White bread

1.5 L	all-purpose flour
15 mL	lard or shortening
15 mL	yeast or 1 yeast cake, softened in 60 mL lukewarm water
30 mL	sugar
10 mL	salt
250 mL	scalded milk
250 mL	boiling water

Put shortening, sugar, and salt in large bowl, or in top of large double boiler. Add liquids. Cool to lukewarm. Add yeast. Stir in 750 mL flour. Mix thoroughly with spoon. Add 500 mL flour, mix, and add remaining flour gradually, using just enough to prevent sticking to the bowl.

Put the last 120 mL of flour on the mixing board or cloth and use some of it to dust the board very lightly, pushing the rest aside to work into the dough if you need it. Turn the ball of dough onto the board. Cover the dough and let it "rest" for 10 minutes. This will make the dough easier to work with. Knead the dough until it becomes elastic. Cover it with a towel and allow it to double in size in a warm place.

Dust the board lightly with some of the flour.

Work ingredients together with your hands. Knead the dough until it becomes elastic.

Put dough into a bowl. Cover with a towel.

Allow dough to double in size in a warm place.

Now have some fun. Punch the dough!

Now for the fun part! Punch the dough, knead it, beat it with your hands for 10 minutes or so. Divide the dough in half. Roll each half into a rectangle. Form dough into loaves. (Warm bread-pans by the fire or in stove before greasing.) Place dough seam side down in greased loaf pans. Brush tops of loaves with butter. Let loaves rise again for about 1½ hours, or until doubled in size.

Preheat oven to 220° C. Do not allow the sides of the pans to touch each other or the sides of the oven. Bake 30–35 minutes or until the bread is brown. Reduce heat to 180° C after 10 minutes. Brush bread again with butter. Knock loaves out of pans and cool on wire racks.

Beat it with your hands!

No! You can't throw it!

Form the dough into loaves.

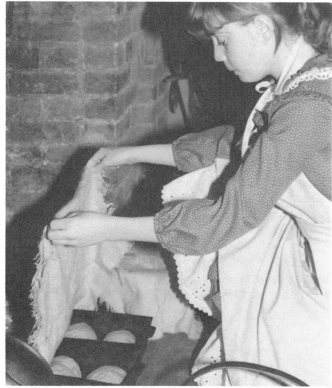

Warm bread pans by fire. Grease pans.
Put loaves into greased pans. Brush tops
of loaves with butter. Let loaves rise
again until double in size.

Place bread far into hot bread oven. Bake
until brown. Remove bread on a peel.
(You can remove your bread from the oven
with oven mitts.)

Fresh homemade bread and butter. Delicious!

Beyond a dog's taste

Not every attempt at baking bread ends as a success story. One little prairie settler was left in charge of cooking and baking when her mother was ill. Her experience, I am sure, was that of many cooks at one time or another when things did not work out "just right."

"I knew how to make yeast bread, or thought I did, but I found I had trouble managing the heat. I put the bread to rise exactly where I had seen Mother put it, but the time was September and the weather getting something cooler.

"The bread would not rise. The next day came and the dough was a pale, flat, lifeless slab, though I turned the pan around and around. Another day came, and I was in despair. My father never noticed anything, or at least said nothing. Not so the young farmhand! As he was going off to work, he stopped in the door and said: 'I guess you'd better keep that pan of dough. Your father can use it when he is mending up that gully down by the pasture next month. He'll want quite a lot of stones.'

"My feelings were hurt beyond repair! I did not keep the pan of dough. Pluto, my dog, and I dug a hole together, and we buried it, for it was by then even past his taste."

Interesting ways to use bread

Now that you have baked your own bread you should use it in interesting ways. Below are some recipes from old children's magazines and cookbooks. All of the recipes are easy enough for those just learning to cook.

Welsh rabbit

Welsh rabbit is a simple and delicious dish for first-time cooks to try. The only ingredients needed are butter, dry mustard, red and black pepper, salt, a piece of cheese, and a slice of bread.

Toast the bread on both sides, butter it, and put it in the oven with just enough heat to keep it warm. Cut about 100 g of cheese into small cubes and put it into a warm frying pan with about 10 mL butter. Stir the cheese as it melts. Mix a dash of red pepper, a dash of salt, and 2 mL of dry mustard in a small bowl. Add about 30 mL of water and stir.

Blend this mixture into the cheese as it melts. When everything is mixed and melted as smooth as very rich cream, pour it over the toast. Dash a little black pepper over the toast, and the rabbit is ready to eat. The whole operation should take less than 10 minutes, including cleaning the frying pan.

Milk toast

Heat 250 mL milk until it is almost boiling. Melt 5 mL butter in a pan and add 5 mL flour. Cook the butter and flour, stirring constantly, until the mixture bubbles a little. Take the butter and flour from the heat and pour one-third of the milk into the butter at a time. Press out any lumps with the back of a spoon. Stir in the remaining milk. Add 1 mL salt and let cook until thick. Keep stirring so the sauce does not stick or burn. Pour sauce over toast.

Old-fashioned flapjacks

Save a bowl of sour milk (about 500 mL), and put any dry pieces of bread left from the table or loaf into it. When this mixture is thick and you want griddle-cakes, break up the bread pieces and add an egg, salt, a few spoonfuls of flour, and about 5mL of baking powder. Toast on a griddle until nicely browned on both sides.

Bread pudding

500 mL	stale bread, cut into small squares
500 mL	milk
30 mL	sugar
2	eggs
2 mL	vanilla
	hot water

Moisten the bread with the hot water. Grease the pudding dish with the butter, and add the moistened bread. Beat the yolks of the eggs, and add the sugar and milk. Pour this over the bread. Beat the whites of the eggs and add 30 mL of sugar. Beat well. Spread this over the top of the pudding. Bake in a moderate oven, about 175° C, for half an hour or until browned. Serve with hard sauce or cream.

Hard sauce

20 mL	soft butter
180 mL	sugar
3 mL	vanilla
1	egg white, beaten stiff

Warm bowl and spoon with boiling water. Cream butter. Add sugar and vanilla. Fold in egg whites. Store in a cool place.

Pumpkin marmalade

Pumpkin marmalade is a tasty spread for fresh bread. The settlers made large batches of everything. The recipe we found for Pumpkin marmalade would have lasted the settlers a long time. We have made the old recipe smaller and simpler. We found we like the new version even better than the old.

400 mL	canned pure pumpkin
180 mL	white sugar
1	lemon, seeds removed, and chopped, including the peel
1	orange, seeds removed, and chopped, including the peel
250 mL	raisins
	dash of salt
5 mL	ginger

Mix all the ingredients except the pumpkin in a saucepan. Heat slowly until sugar has melted. Add pumpkin. Simmer for 40-60 minutes until flavors have blended and rinds are softened.

Making butter the old-fashioned way

The fresh milk that was to be made into butter was put into a stone crock in a cool room for a day or two. The cream in the milk rose to the top. The cream was skimmed and put into a churn. It was important that the churn and utensils were sparkling clean. Butter absorbs the smells around it when it is being made.

Samantha churns the butter by rolling the stick between her fingers. She also pumps it up and down to beat the cream.

She checks to see if butter is forming yet. Some small grains start to appear on the bottom of the stick.

The butter is ready when small pieces of it start to float in the liquid. The liquid that does not form into butter is called buttermilk.

The buttermilk is strained from the butter. The butter is washed over and over again until the water poured on it stays clear.

Andrea uses a wooden spatula to squeeze the buttermilk out of the butter. She needs to wash this butter one more time.

When the last bit of liquid is poured off, pure butter remains in the trough. The butter is then salted. Sometimes a drop of carrot juice is added for color.

Fresh butter ready to be spread on homemade bread! It took Samantha and Andrea only about an hour to churn and wash their butter. Not bad for a first try!

Doggone tiring

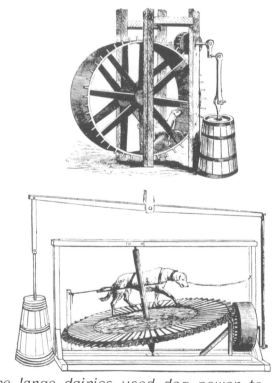

The hardest part of making the butter was staying seated on this tippy stool!

Some large dairies used dog power to churn butter.

These cheese curds have been salted. Next, they will be packed into a cheese press and left to age. The longer the cheese ages, the stronger it will taste.

Enough cheese to please

Milk from the evening and morning milkings was mixed in a tub and heated near the fire until it was almost body temperature. Rennet was stirred into the milk. (Rennet came from the inner lining of a calf's stomach.) In about half an hour the milk turned into *curds* which felt like jelly. The liquid that did not curdle was called *whey*. The whey was drained from the curds. The curd was cut into small squares, left to sit for fifteen minutes,

and was heated again. Salt was worked into the curd and the curd was packed into a cheese press. (There were many kinds of presses, but the early settlers put the curd into a simple hoop and added pressure to the curd with weights.) The hoop and weight pressed the curd into a hard round cheese which was stored in a dark room and rubbed regularly with butter. The longer the cheese was stored, the stronger it tasted.

47

"Hasty pudding? I call it 'mush'!"

Workday meals

The settlers worked hard in the fields or at their crafts. They needed to eat enough food to supply them with all the energy needed to get their daily work done. One settler recalls her daily meals in the following story.

"Breakfast was at 5 a.m. There was Johnny Cake or cornbread (see p.25) and mush. All human beings need mush to start the day, only some call it 'stirabout' and some call it 'porridge.' We made it out of yellow cornmeal."

Hasty pudding

The "mush" the settler talked about was also known as Hasty Pudding.

750 mL	*water*
5 mL	*salt*
200 mL	*cornmeal*

Put water and salt in a saucepan. Bring to a boil. Sprinkle cornmeal into the water a little at a time, stirring constantly to prevent lumps. Cook 25 minutes. Serve with milk, maple syrup, or fruit.

The flapjack contest

"After the mush came flapjacks in great numbers. Flapjacks are small pancakes done on a griddle and eaten with molasses. They must be made quickly and be very hot. A working man will eat 20 to 30 and smilingly ask for more. Imagine a small child standing over a very hot stove, flap-jacking for dear life at dawn.

"There is a legend in our family that once I offered, or received, a challenge from one of our workmen to cook as many as he could eat. He was a big fellow, very strong and very lazy. But on this occasion he outdid himself. I fell out of the race at the seventy-third flapjack, as he held up his plate for more." (See recipe for Flap-jacks, p.43.)

The hired hand loves flapjacks!

Hunger signal

The settlers called their lunch "dinner" and their dinner "supper" because at noon they had their biggest meal. At about 12 o'clock the settlers working in the fields waved their handkerchiefs to show that they were hungry!

"A signal from the cornfield set me to work on the dinner. There was usually chicken pot-pie, sweet potatoes, corn-bread, and water to drink. Supper was what was left over from dinner, all cold."

Chicken pot-pie

	pastry for two-crust pie (see p.21)
30 mL	flour
30 mL	butter or margarine
5 mL	salt
2 mL	pepper
2 mL	thyme
120 mL	chicken broth (made from a cube)
120 mL	half-and-half cream
500 mL	small chicken or turkey pieces
250 mL	mixed peas and carrots
250 mL	chopped onion, browned in butter
120 mL	corn

Heat oven to 220° C. Prepare pastry as directed. Melt butter in a large saucepan. Stir in flour, salt, pepper, and thyme, and simmer until mixture is smooth. Remove from heat and add chicken broth and cream. Heat until bubbly, stirring constantly for 1 minute. Add chicken and vegetables. Pour into pastry-lined pie dish and cover with sheet of pastry. Seal and flute (pinch) edges. Slash top sheet of pastry in several places to allow steam to escape. Bake 40-45 minutes or until golden brown.

The dinner vegetables were boiled together in one pot.

A kiss for a colored ear of corn! These settlers are working up quite an appetite for the supper that awaits them.

Every bee was followed by a huge feast. The neighbor, left, missed all the work, but he is still invited in for a bite to eat.

Hearty food for hard workers

Bees were work parties. Many bees were held to harvest, prepare, and preserve foods. Sugaring-off, corn-husking, apple bees, taffy pulls, and threshing bees were all "food" bees. The settlers also ate a great deal of food. The reward at the end of every bee was a huge feast for all the workers. So whether the settlers prepared food or made quilts, the bees all ended at the same place - the table. The hosts and hostesses of the bees did not just make sandwiches either! There were roasts, pies, and stews of every kind along with breads, cakes, vegetables, and tarts. One could hardly talk about a bee without mentioning the main event - FOOD! A settler described the food served at a corn-husking bee:

The board groaned beneath the feast

"The feast was spread in a large shed, the table being formed of two broad boards laid together and supported by rude carpenter's stools. The board was covered with an indescribable variety of roast and boiled fish, flesh, and fowl.

"Besides venison, pork, chickens, ducks, and fish of all kinds, cooked in a variety of ways, there was a number of pumpkin, raspberry, cherry, and currant jams, with fresh butter and cheese, maple molasses, preserves, and pickled cucumbers, besides tea and coffee."

Who will get the last apple of the harvest?

The apple harvest

Wise settlers brought apple seedlings with them to plant as soon as they arrived. It took many years for seedlings to grow big enough to produce a good crop of fruit. The crop of a mature apple orchard was put to many uses. When the apples were not eaten raw, dried, or cooked, they were made into jam, jelly, applesauce, apple butter, or cider.

The apple bee

The apple bee was a special event at harvest time. A family invited their neighbors to help peel and core most of the apple crop. Apples were pared either by hand or with small paring machines. The families and friends at the apple bee worked hard, but they also played. They sang songs and told stories while they kept warm around an outdoor fire. The fire was also used to cook the apple butter and applesauce.

Bruised apples made good cider

The "windfall" apples that had blown from the trees and had been bruised were used to make cider. These "second-best" apples were pressed at home or were piled into a wagon and taken to the cider mill. At the mill the apples were crushed in a large press which squeezed the juice from them.

Windfall apples made good cider.

A little love, a little talk, and a lot of food make the apple bees more fun than work.

Apple butter and applesauce

The settlers saved some of their cider for serving to visitors and serving at bees, but much of it was turned into apple butter. The cider was boiled for two days in a large kettle hung over the fire. Fresh apples were added to the boiling cider to thicken it into butter.

Applesauce was made by cooking apple pieces instead of cider. The applesauce and apple butter were both stirred all day and all night as they cooked. The adults took turns turning a paddle in the pots to keep the sauce or butter from burning.

Some of the apples pared and cored at apple bees were dried in the shape of rings. Drying the apples preserved them for a long time. The pieces of apple were dipped into boiling water so that they kept a fresh color even when they dried. The rings were strung on a thread or placed on spikes. ➤

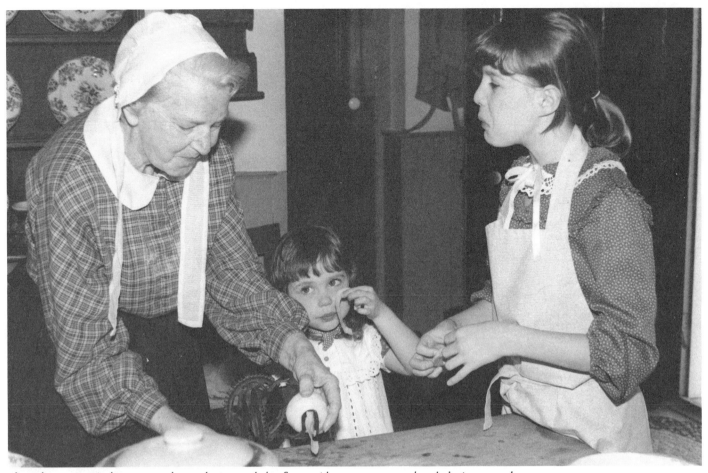

Apples must be cored and pared before they are cooked into applesauce.

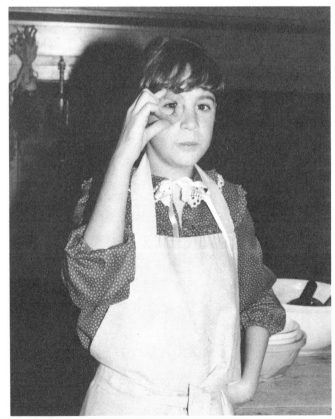

Two of these and I'd have a pair of glasses!

Apple doll heads are easy and fun to make. Now to add a body!

What can we make with flour and apples? You guessed it, apple pie!

Baked apples

There were other interesting ways to cook apples. Baked apples were a great favorite with children. They were easy to make. They could be eaten alone as a dessert, or as a side dish for pork, ham, or turkey.

Wipe large apples (as many as you require). Core with knife or apple corer. Place in earthenware or enamel dish. Fill center of each with sugar. (If you want an extra-rich dessert treat, combine raisins, nutmeg, and cinnamon with the sugar.) Pour water into the dish. Allow 30 mL for each apple. Bake in a hot oven for an hour, or until soft.

Apple snow

Apple snow was a treat that made children's eyes sparkle with glee.

Pare and grate apples. Drop grated apple immediately into very cold water so that it does not turn brown. Drain water from grated apple. Cook in a heavy saucepan slowly until soft. Measure apple sauce. For every 250 mL use 60 mL powdered sugar and the white of one egg, well beaten. Add a spoonful of each in turn to apples until all is used, stirring in lightly each time. Add a drop of vanilla for each 250 mL of apples. Serve with whipped cream.

Apple crumb cake

"Thickly grease a pie dish with a layer (about 1 cm) of butter. Throw in a large quantity of bread crumbs, as many as will stick when pressed well on the butter. Have some apples already stewed and sweetened. (You can stew apples by paring and slicing 8-10 of them and cooking them until they are soft, but not mushy.) Fill the dish with the apples. Put 30 ml of butter in bits on top and cover over with bread crumbs to a 2 cm thickness. Put into a hot oven (220° C) until brown and crusty. When done, pass a knife around the outside and turn the cake out of the pan. Sprinkle sugar over the top and glaze by placing the cake under the broiler for a few minutes, until the sugar melts." Watch carefully or the sugar will burn! If the cake is eaten hot, a scoop of vanilla ice cream on top tastes wonderful.

While his sad friend waits, a small dog turns a huge roast.

This picture clearly shows the swinging crane attached to the inside wall of the fireplace. Pot hooks dangle from it. You can also see the andirons.

Bake Kettle
Broiler
Basting Pan

Kathleen winds the jack the same way she would wind a clock. The meat is then hung on the hook. It will turn slowly over the fire and roast evenly.

The dangers of the fireplace

The center of the early kitchen was the fireplace. The first fireplaces were made of logs covered with mud or clay. They were dangerous because if the logs caught on fire, the whole house would go up in flames. A crossbar or lugpole rested on ledges built into the two sides of the early fireplace. Cooking pots and kettles hung from this pole. The early settlers cut their lugpoles from wet, green wood. These wooden poles would sooner or later dry up and burn through, causing spoiled dinners, and sometimes, much worse. The kettles and pots crashed down into the fire. Those who were sitting too close to the fireplace came away with bad burns and broken bones.

Mary O'Brien, a settler in 1828, was just preparing supper for guests when her lugpole decided to give way. Here is her story.

A cooking catastrophe

"I had just finished the first stage of my cooking when accidents began to happen. My little roast of pork was dangling before the fire at the end of a string. I was unable to roast it as usual in my all-purpose bake kettle. A loaf of bread was happily rising and baking there.

"I looked over to the bake kettle, and lo and behold, its lid was raised upwards by the unexpected rise of my bread. The bread had grown so large, it was threatening to run down the sides of the kettle and into the ashes. Quickly I cut some dough from the top of my loaf and placed it before the fire on a plate. There I hoped it would bake into delicious biscuits. (I was quite proud of my quick work.) Of course the frying pan would have been the natural place to make them, but that was being used as a dripping pan for the pork. Oh, who can number up the uses of a bake kettle and frying pan!

"I had just turned from rescuing my bread, when suddenly the pole above gave way. On it had been resting a saucepan containing rooster and cabbage stew. The stew spilled all over my biscuits. The biscuits were spoiled. However, luckily, the plate saved my old rooster from being buried in the ashes and I was then able to save my stew."

Hooks, cranes, trammels, and trivets

As soon as there was a blacksmith in the community, the settlers had their fireplace poles and utensils made of iron. The lugpole soon disappeared. Instead, the blacksmiths now fashioned a new type of bar called a *swinging crane*. The crane was anchored into the fireplace wall. It could swing in and out of the fireplace. The kettles and pots hung over the fire from hooks attached to the crane. A system of hooks that could be moved up or down was called a *trammel*. The crane allowed the cook to stir the stew without having to lean into the fire. The trammel allowed the cook to regulate the heat reaching the pot. The pot could be moved down for more heat or up for less. The frying pans and cooking utensils all had long handles so that the ends of the handles would be away from the fire and the cook's hands would not be burned. All of the pots and kettles had legs so that they could easily sit over the coals or logs in the fireplace. *Trivets* were three-legged stands on which pans could be placed into the fire. They came in different heights.

The jogging dog

The *andirons* held the logs in place. Another name for andirons was *fire-dogs*. One type of fire-dog was made especially to hold the turnspit. The turnspit was turned by hand or by a poor dog. The dog had to run inside a wheel to turn the spit. It was a hot, tiring, and thankless job.

Jacks of all kinds

Joints of meat were roasted either on a spit or on a rope. The rope was hung from the ceiling in front of the fire. Someone had to keep turning the roast around so that all sides would be cooked. *Jacks* were invented for this purpose. A jack was a small machine with a hook at its bottom. The roast hung from the hook over the fire. The jack turned the roast around. *Clock-jacks* were wound the same way as one would wind a clock. The roast would be turned around over the fire for the length of time the spring in the jack took to unwind. *Smoke-jacks* turned the meat according to how hot the fire and how much smoke was reaching the jack.

The indoor bread ovens were usually built into the side of the fireplace, as shown in this picture. A smoke passage was built in to connect with the fireplace chimney.

Brick oven bread-baking

The *bread oven* was built into the side of the fireplace. It was made of bricks. The oven was filled with wood or coals which were burned. The fire heated the bricks. The coals and ashes were swept out. When the oven cooled down a bit, the bread was put in for baking. The bread was placed into the oven on a long-handled wooden shovel called a *peel*. The heat from the bricks baked the bread. Many bread ovens were located outdoors. Some homes had both indoor and outdoor bread ovens. The one on the fireplace was used in winter, and the one outdoors was used in summer.

Outdoor ovens and summer kitchens

As well as summer bake ovens, many settlers also had summer kitchens. Summer kitchens were either just outside the regular kitchen, or were built on as additions outside the wall of the house. In this way, the cooking did not heat the rest of the house in summer. Summer kitchens came

after stoves were invented. In the summer the stoves could be moved out into the summer kitchen. In the winter this room was used for storage. Some of the wealthier settlers had their kitchens in separate buildings away from the main house. Cooking accidents and fires then would not burn the house down.

Taking the hot bread from the oven on a peel.

The summer kitchen was added on outside the regular kitchen. The back of the kitchen fireplace shows through. The stove was moved out into the summer kitchen in hot weather so that the rest of the house would not get hotter.

An outdoor bread oven.

The first stoves were built low so that the huge iron pots would be at the right height for cooking. This stove was built into the old kitchen fireplace.

Cooking was made much easier with the coming of the stove.

Stoves for simpler cooking

The first stoves were placed into the fireplace so that the smoke could escape up the chimney. Later a system of pipes took the smoke up through the chimney. Stoves were sometimes as dangerous as fireplaces. If the pipes were not cleaned regularly a fire would start in the chimney. Stoves used up much of the oxygen in a room. When all the windows and doors were shut tight in the winter so that no fresh air came into the house, the settlers had to breathe bad air.

For cooking, however, stoves were a great improvement over fireplaces. The early stoves were made low so that the settlers could use their big iron cooking pots from the fireplace. These huge pots would be at the right height for cooking if placed on a low stove. In later times, as the pots and pans were made smaller and lighter, the stoves were built higher.

Some of the more expensive stoves contained ovens, warming closets for keeping cooked food warm, and *rotisseries* for evenly roasting joints of meat. A rotisserie was a device used for turning meat as it roasted.

The settlers imagined the kitchens of their future to be large, useful, and very fancy.

Kitchens of the future

Settlers often wondered about the future, as we do today. When we think of food in the future, we imagine taking a pill to replace a meal. We do not think of kitchens, we think of computers preparing whole meals in seconds. The settlers thought the opposite when they imagined kitchens of the future. They thought of big fancy rooms and huge cooking machines. The two old drawings on this page illustrate how the settlers imagined the kitchens of their future would look. Why do you think they were so wrong?

This future stove would be able to cook a whole pig at a time. The settlers thought that wood would still be the source of energy in the future.

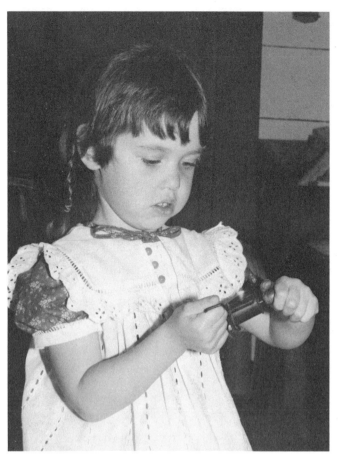

A little gadget for crushing nutmeg.

Sugar was sold in cones in the early days. These tongs were used for taking off the amount needed.

Gadgets galore

There are many interesting things to find in a pioneer kitchen. Here are a few examples of old gadgets.

Cinnamon sticks from the spice shelf smell terrific.

What might the settlers have put into this mold?

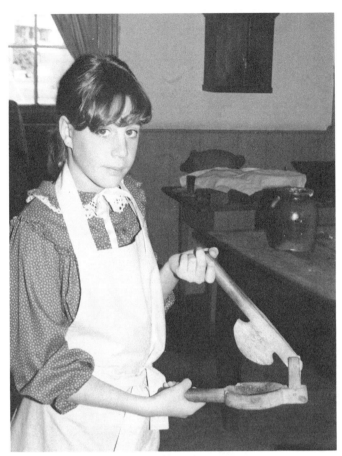

A device for squeezing lemons.

A lard press for smoothing flower petals? Well, why not!

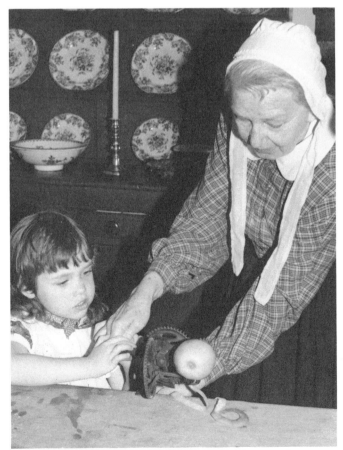

An apple corer and peeler made paring apples quick and easy.

Herbs were ground into powder by a mortar and pestle.

The bench is full of fish caught from the sea. After it is cleaned and scaled, the fish will be dried in the sun and wind. Some of it will be smoked after it is dried.

Keeping food from spoiling

Making pemmican

Settlers had to preserve their fresh meat so that they could eat it through the year. They did not have reliable ways of freezing food until later. The easiest way to preserve meat in the early days was to dry it. The settlers learned how to make *pemmican* from the Indians. They cut beef or buffalo meat into thin strips and dried the strips slowly in the sun and wind or by a fire. When the meat was dry, it could be stored in strips or pounded into a powder with a stone. The powder was mixed with other foods, such as berries, for extra flavor. Pemmican could be kept a long time. The drying method sealed in the meat's juices. Pemmican was sometimes served with scrambled eggs. Water could be added to it to make an instant soup or stew.

Drying fish

Fish was dried in the same way as meat. It was cleaned, scaled, and the backbone was removed. It was wiped dry and laid on a board. After being salted, the fish was washed, strung on a willow wand, and hung to dry in the sun and wind. The fish could also be smoked after it was dried. An easy meal could be prepared by soaking the fish in warm water for a few hours before boiling or frying it.

Settlers built smokehouses of logs, bricks, or stones. Log smokehouses easily caught on fire, so brick and stone ones were preferred.

Pickling, smoking, and potting meat

Animals were usually butchered in the early winter. The scraps were used to make sausages. Some of the meat was frozen. However, if the settlers wanted to be sure of a meat supply in the warm months, they pickled most of their fresh meat. A hundred kilograms was often preserved at one time. After the pork or beef was cut and trimmed from a carcass, it was rubbed with a mixture of sugar, saltpeter, and salt. Bacon was packed in a tray and beef was packed in a barrel with a stone weight on top of it. Every few days the meat was moved so that all the pieces were soaked. The meat could be left in the pickling mixture for as much as a year and then used for cooking. Then, if the settlers wished, they could also smoke or dry the pickled meat.

Often the meat was taken out of the pickle in the spring. It was washed and hung in the smokehouse. The smokehouse was a small building usually built in the yard near the brick oven. The walls of the log smokehouse were covered with *creosote*, a grease made from coal tar which preserved the wood. Log smokehouses easily caught on fire, so later pioneers built them from brick or stone. In the center of the smokehouse was a fire pit dug into the earth floor and lined with stones or bricks. The settlers burned green hardwoods such as oak, alder, or hickory because these woods burned slowly and gave the best flavor to the meat. Sometimes corncobs were used as fuel in smokehouses. The meat was smoked for as long as a week.

Before the settlers built smokehouses, they hung their roasts in their chimneys. The roasts were high above the fire to prevent them from cooking as they were smoked.

Potting was another method used to preserve meat and fish, but it was harder work than salting or smoking because the meat or fish had to be pounded into a paste before it was potted. The paste was mixed with spices, put into a pot, and covered with melted butter so that the mixture was sealed.

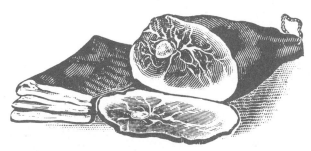

Smoked ham.

Ice was cut out of the lake in blocks. The settler will go to the ice house and pack the ice in sawdust. The sawdust will insulate the ice, preventing the summer heat from melting it.

Preserving vegetables and fruit

Pickling was also used to preserve vegetables. Cucumbers, onions, and melons were put into wooden barrels and covered with brine. Brine was a mixture of water, vinegar, salt, and spices. The brine gave the vegetables a strong flavor as it preserved them.

Fruits were preserved in jams and jellies. Sweeteners such as honey and sugar were mixed with fruit, cider, and cinnamon. The mixture was sealed in a crock. Melted mutton fat was used as the seal, and leather or an animal bladder was stretched over the crock to keep out dust.

Root cellars

Many fruits and vegetables would last the winter when they were stored in the root cellar. Root cellars were built under houses or into the sides of hills. The root cellar was below the frost line so the fruits and vegetables would not freeze in the winter. Because the root cellar was deep in the ground, the food was kept cool in summer.

In the latter half of the nineteenth century, settlers were able to buy some meats, vegetables, and fruits in cans. Canning was a new way of preserving food.

Cider, pickled meat, pickled vegetables, fruit preserves, and eggs were also kept in the root cellar. Eggs could be stored and kept fresh. They were coated with fat or melted wax, and packed in ashes, sawdust, or straw.

Springhouses and ice houses

Some pioneer homesteads had springhouses where food was kept. Springhouses were small sheds built over cold, running springs. Butter and cream in crocks and jugs could be put directly into the cold water. Some settlers lowered food in pails into their water wells to keep food cold. Others used ice houses. Ice houses were built half above and half below the ground and had good drains. Ice was cut and carried from the river in the winter. The ice was packed in sawdust. In the winter, of course, the settlers only had to put their food outside the doors of their houses to keep it cold.

These pigs were brought to the city market from the country. They will be sold whole and frozen.

Will it be venison steak or a whole pig for Thanksgiving? These city settlers are having trouble making up their minds.

Buying food

The settlers who lived in or near the cities could buy much of their meat at the local market or butcher's store. They could buy a frozen pig or a turkey for Christmas dinner. The meat came from the farms to the cities fresh in the summer and frozen in the winter. When the settlers bought their meat, they had to clean it and cut it themselves. They usually had to buy a whole animal rather than only chicken wings or pork chops.

If this chef had used the custard powder advertised, he would not be lying there with egg on his face. New products such as the one above made life easier for the cook.

Selling food through advertising

Other foods as well as meat were available for sale. These could be found at the grocery stores. In the latter half of the nineteenth century, city settlers could buy a number of packaged and canned goods. Oysters and clams could be bought in cans, and oatmeal could be bought in boxes instead of barrels. These prepared foods were still considered luxuries, but more and more of them started to appear on the shelves. As manufacturers produced new goods, they wanted people to know about them. Advertisements were placed in newspapers and magazines. When people read the advertisements which described how good these products were, they asked their local store owners to stock the products on the shelves.

This cocoa company did well to advertise its product. It is one of the biggest companies selling cocoa today.

Oatmeal was not new to the settlers. The box was, however.

Another cocoa company advertises to get its share of the market.

"Beef tea" was a popular drink for babies or people who were ill. With beef extract it could be made quickly and easily by adding some hot water.

Louise found out the hard way that cooking does not come naturally. Her husband is showing her a chicken she cooked with the head, feet and some feathers still on it.

Food for thought

As the settlers grew wealthier they could afford to hire servants to do much of their work. The first job most housewives wanted to hire a servant for was cooking. Some women felt that cooking was a terrible job that should be done by others.

In the homes of the wealthy settlers, girls were not even taught how to cook. Their mothers were sure that their daughters would always have servants. If the daughters married men who could not afford servants, these new brides were lost in the kitchen. In one situation a bride married a man who bought his own farm. The bride and groom moved to the country. The wife did not know how to cook, but was eager to learn. She rode to the general store with her shopping list. She asked to buy enough ingredients for one cake. Everyone in the store laughed. They were used to buying enough food to last a month, not just enough to bake a cake!

In another instance, a woman named Louise caught her servant trying on one of her dresses. Louise was furious! She sent the woman packing. However, now she was faced with a big problem. She did not know how to cook dinner. Louise felt that it would be easy enough. After all, that wretched servant could do it! By the time Louise's husband came home that night, the kitchen was a disaster! Food was spilled all over the table and floor.

It took Louise three weeks to find another servant. Her family nearly starved.

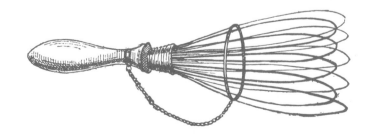

These girls are learning more than just how to cook. They receive lessons in nutrition, chemistry, and anatomy in this domestic science class.

Louise's situation, and that of the young bride in the story above, was not unusual. Two sisters, Catherine Beecher and Harriet Beecher Stowe, came to the rescue. They believed cooking should be looked at in a whole new way. The Beecher sisters felt that women should be just as professional about homemaking as doctors were about medicine. Catherine Beecher started a school that taught homemaking as a science. Both sisters wrote books and magazine articles teaching women how to run their homes.

They gave women the knowledge of chemistry, physics, and biology necessary to run a good home and care for a family. Soon domestic science classes opened in towns and cities. Women began to take pride in the role of homemaker. They no longer had to ask their husbands to fix things around the home. They did it themselves. Instead of considering homemaking to be an unworthy occupation, women felt proud to be doing a job which required a great deal of knowledge. And after all, what could have been more important than the business of raising and feeding a family?

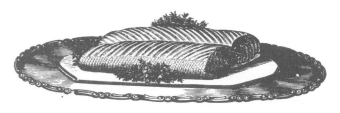

No speaking, smelling, spitting, spilling, or smacking

Mother glares at Harold for having such bad manners. He asked for some chicken instead of waiting for it to be offered.

Licking one's plate was a definite no-no.

The earliest settlers were very strict with their children. The rules for behavior were really hard for a child to follow. Children were not even allowed to sit at the table. They had to stand behind the adults and could eat only what was passed to them from the plates of the grownups. Later, children could sit at the table, but only after the blessing and after they were given permission. They could not speak unless spoken to, and if they wanted a dish passed to them, they could not ask for it. They had to wait until it was offered.

Children were thought rude if they looked at someone else who was eating. They could not bite off a piece of bread, but had to break it into bite-sized pieces. Singing and fidgeting were forbidden. Smacking the lips or even breathing too loudly was considered bad manners. There were rules for eating meat. Children were not allowed to turn a piece of meat over on their plates or to smell it. Licking one's plate was strictly forbidden!

The sloppy settler

Below is a description of a settler who grew up with bad table manners.

"When his tea or coffee is handed to him, he spreads his handkerchief upon his knees, scalds his mouth, drops either the cup or saucer, and spills the tea or coffee in his lap. At dinner, he seats himself upon the edge of his chair, at so great a distance from the table, that he drops his meat between his plate and his mouth; he holds his knife, fork, and spoon differently from other people, eats with his knife, and picks his teeth with his fork.

"In cutting his meat, he splashes the sauce over everybody's clothes. He generally spots himself all over; his elbows are in the next person's plate; and he is up to the knuckles in soup and grease. If he drinks, he coughs in his glass and sprinkles his drink over the whole table."

Elbows on the table, elbows in the air; both of these will get you a very angry stare!

Mr. Foxtrot and his cat have different ideas about what is good to eat.

"Forget grace. Let's dig in!" says this bad-mannered guest.

Sardine sandwiches and ginger drops are dainty dishes to offer at a tea party.

Tea party recipes

Tea parties were very popular with the settlers. Children of all ages held tea parties for their classmates, friends, dolls, and even pets. Adults also had many tea parties. Adults served tiny sandwiches, biscuits, and cakes. Children usually served cookies or sweets. We have found some interesting recipes for both children's and adults' tea parties.

Sardine sandwiches

Bone and pass through a sieve twelve sardines, the yolks of two hard-boiled eggs, and enough butter to give the mixture a paste-like texture. Add some finely chopped parsley, and season with black pepper and cayenne. Mix it all well together.

Cut some slices of thin bread and butter and spread the sardine mixture on each slice. Cut the sandwiches into oblong shapes, and serve with watercress or lettuce in the middle.

This recipe can also be made with tuna-fish. The ingredients could be mixed in a blender or food processor. For extra zest, you could add some minced onion and a little prepared mustard and paprika.

Ginger drops

250 mL   *sugar*
10 mL   *ginger*
               the white of 1 egg, well beaten

Mix well, and drop on white paper with a good large teaspoon. Bake in a moderate (180° C) oven for about 10 minutes. The drops are done as soon as they can easily be taken off the paper.

"If you are good, Pussy, you can try some of the thimble biscuits Dolly and I just baked."

Thimble biscuits for tiny tea-toddlers

250 mL	*flour*
20 mL	*butter*
120 mL	*milk*
10 mL	*baking powder*
2 mL	*salt*

Preheat oven to 220° C. Grease cookie sheet. Sift flour, baking powder and salt three times. Rub butter lightly into flour. Pour milk on gradually, mixing all the while, until a soft dough is formed. Turn the dough onto a well-floured board. Roll it with a rolling pin to the thickness of 1 cm. Use a large thimble (or small cookie cutter) and cut biscuits as close to each other as possible. Place on cookie sheet a little distance apart. Bake 5 minutes. Serve to your friends, dolls, dog, or cat.

Apple pie tastes great anytime.

Turning the dasher is hard work. Joe deserves his reward.

Cold, sweet, and sticky

Children looked forward to making ice cream with the help of their friends. They could use the fresh berries or fruit they had picked. They could argue about who would turn the dasher in order to make the ice cream smooth. After the ice cream was made, one of the children would be lucky enough to be able to lick the *dasher*.

The earliest settlers used a simple pail and wooden tub in which to make their ice cream. In later days freezer churns were invented. The cream was put into the container of the churn and the container was surrounded with ice. Inside the churn was the dasher which turned and smoothed the ice cream as it froze. The children took turns working the dasher until the ice cream was ready.

Freezer churn ice cream

500 mL	fruit of your choice, such as strawberries or peaches
120 mL	white sugar
620 mL	heavy cream
	dash of salt

Crush the fruit a little bit. Add the sugar and salt to the fruit and mix well. Put in freezer of the fridge so that the flavor gets stronger. Pour the cream into the freezer churn and cover it with the dasher handle poking through. Pack the space surrounding the container with crushed ice and coarse salt (6 parts of ice to 1 part of salt). Turn the dasher slowly until the cream starts to thicken (about 10 minutes). Add the fruit and churn again, but more quickly this time, until the cream is frozen. Remove the dasher and pack the ice cream into a container. You may eat it right away but the taste improves if you put it in the freezer for a few hours.

Easy banana ice cream

If you do not have an ice-cream maker, don't despair! You can make ice cream in an ice-cube tray in your freezer. Here is an easy recipe for you to follow.

3	very ripe bananas
	juice of 1 lemon
125 mL	granulated sugar
250 mL	heavy cream
2.5 mL	salt

In one bowl, mash up the bananas and add lemon juice and sugar. In another bowl, beat cream until stiff and add salt. Combine the banana mixture with the whipped cream and mix well. Pour into ice-cube tray. Freeze until hard. Add fresh fruit or whipped topping to individual servings.

Are these young couples pulling for candy, pulling for Saint Catherine, or pulling for love?

Taffy for a pulling party

Taffy pulling was a social event among both children and adults. Children invited their friends over to help make, pull, and eat the taffy. Adults also held taffy-pulling parties. It was a custom among the French settlers to hold pulling parties on the Feast of Saint Catherine. Saint Catherine was a martyr who died on November 25, 307 A.D. She became the patron saint for unmarried girls. On November 25 of each year, the unmarried men in the community were invited to the homes of the unmarried women for an evening of fun, feasting, and taffy pulling. Taffy pulling gave the young people a chance to get to know each other better. Some settlers ended up marrying their taffy-pulling partners.

Plain taffy

750 mL	white sugar
120 mL	vinegar
120 mL	water
30 mL	butter

Mix the ingredients and bring them to a boil in a big pot. After about 10 minutes of boiling the taffy, test it by dropping a spoonful into cold water. Probably the taffy will only dissolve and make the water muddy, but it may already form little soft balls. Keep testing the taffy every few minutes. The longer you cook it, the harder it will be when it is cooled. It is just ready for pulling if the syrup forms a hard ball when thrown into cold water.

Half the joy of making taffy is having friends over to share the fun.

As soon as the taffy has boiled long enough, pour it into buttered pans. You can flavor it with vanilla or maple syrup just before you pour it. Let the taffy cool until you can handle it, then butter your hands. Pull until the taffy is a white color. Cut the pulled taffy into pieces with sharp scissors.

Molasses taffy

250 mL	molasses
250 mL	white sugar
250 mL	brown sugar
120 mL	corn syrup
120 mL	water
15 mL	butter
15 mL	vinegar
15 mL	baking soda
	a few drops of vanilla

Put all the ingredients except soda in a pot. Heat until the mixture "candies" when tested in cold water (as in Plain Taffy recipe). Add soda and mix well. Generously butter a platter. Pour the taffy onto the platter. Pull candy with both hands or between yourself and a friend until the candy is a golden color. Cut into small pieces and wrap in waxed paper.

Dishes brought from different lands

Menu.

Irish Soda Bread

Dandelion Greens
Salad

Scotch Eggs

French Pea Soup

German
Cod and Potatoes

Ukrainian
Cabbage Rolls

Dutch
Apple Pudding

Minute Champagne

The settlers came to the New World from many European countries. They brought with them different traditions, ways of dress, and many recipes for their food. We have chosen recipes which have come from different countries. They have all been adapted to modern kitchens. Each recipe can be used alone. However, together they make an entire meal from salad and appetizer to dessert and drink. Enjoy your "heritage" meal.

Irish soda bread

500 mL	flour
15 mL	sugar
7.5 mL	baking powder
2.5 mL	baking soda
100 mL	butter
200 mL	raisins
200 mL	milk
15 mL	vinegar

Preheat oven to 185° C. Sift flour, baking powder, baking soda, sugar, and salt together. Cut butter into flour mixture with two knives until butter is well blended. Stir in raisins. Add vinegar to milk. Add sour milk to the other ingredients while quickly stirring with a fork. Knead dough lightly on a floured board. Shape into a round loaf and place in a well-greased, 20 cm round cake pan. Score the top in the shape of a cross. Bake in a preheated oven for 30-40 minutes or until golden brown.

Dandelion greens salad

Dandelions were not thought of as weeds in the days of the settlers. The Indians taught the settlers that dandelions were a valuable vegetable. The settlers also made wine and a coffee-like beverage from dandelions. Below is an old recipe for a salad made of dandelion greens.

800 mL	dandelion greens
3	hard-boiled eggs
4	slices of bacon, fried until crisp

Pick fresh dandelions with young and tender leaves which have not been sprayed with weed killer. Wash the leaves and set on a towel to drain. Boil eggs and fry bacon until crisp. Drain fat from bacon and break the meat into small pieces. Toss the ingredients together in a bowl. Serve with dressing of your choice or squeeze a fresh lemon over the salad.

Scotch eggs

8	hard-boiled eggs
500 g	sausage meat
2	eggs, slightly beaten
	bread crumbs, enough to coat eggs
	lard or oil for frying
	salt and pepper to taste

Cook eggs until hard-boiled by placing them in a pot of warm water. Cook them slowly on low heat for about 30 minutes. Remove from heat and put eggs in cold water until cooled. Remove the shells. Dip eggs in seasoned flour and mold sausage meat around the egg. Dip in beaten eggs and coat with bread crumbs. Deep-fry in lard or oil until brown. Cut lengthwise in halves.

French pea soup

500 g	dried green peas
250 g	salt pork
2.5 L	water
3	onions, chopped
3	carrots, sliced into cubes
3	bay leaves
100 mL	celery, chopped
60 mL	parsley, chopped
5 mL	savory

Wash and drain peas and put in a soup pot with the other ingredients. Boil for 2 minutes. Remove from heat and let cool for a few hours. Boil a second time. Reduce heat and simmer for $1\frac{1}{2}$ hours or until the peas are soft.

German cod and potatoes

500 g	codfish
300 mL	salt pork pieces
250 mL	cream
5	large potatoes
1	onion, cut up in slices
	pepper to taste
	salt to taste

Peel potatoes and cut into chunks. Cook until about half done. Add fish and cook with the potatoes until potatoes are done. Fry salt pork until brown. Pour off most of the fat, leaving approximately 10 mL in which to fry the onion. Add the onion and brown it with the pork. Add cream. Drain fish and potatoes. Pour cream, onion, and salt pork mixture on top.

Ukrainian cabbage rolls

500 mL	boiling water
500 mL	uncooked rice
10 mL	salt
60 mL	butter
	salt to taste
	pepper to taste
1	onion, finely chopped
1	cabbage
300 mL	tomato juice, seasoned with salt and pepper
30 mL	butter

Preheat oven to 180° C. Boil water, rice, and salt in a pan. Remove pan from heat and leave it so the rice can absorb the water. Melt butter in frying pan and lightly brown the onion in the butter.

Combine rice and onions and season with salt and pepper. Leave the mixture to cool. Core cabbage and place in a deep pan, cored side down. Completely cover the cabbage with boiling water. Let stand until the leaves are soft enough to wrap around filling. Drain cabbage and gently separate the leaves. Cut off the hard, thick parts of the leaves. Spoon filling onto each leaf and roll it up. Place the cabbage rolls side by side and in layers in a buttered oven dish. Mix the tomato juice and butter and pour the mix over the rolls. Bake at 180° C for $1\frac{1}{2}$-2 hours.

Dutch apple pudding

500 mL	flour
30 mL	butter
60 mL	honey
10 mL	baking powder
2 mL	salt
4	apples, peeled and cut in thin slices
1	egg

Preheat oven to 200° C. Beat egg and add to milk. In another bowl, mix flour, baking powder, and salt. Mix the butter into the flour mixture. Pour the milk and egg into the butter and flour and mix quickly. Spread the dough 1.5 cm thick in a square, buttered cake pan. Stick the apple pieces in and on top of the dough. Drip the honey on top. Bake at 200° C for 30 minutes. Serve with cream.

Minute champagne

For those of you who are too young to enjoy the real thing, Minute Champagne is guaranteed to tickle your nose with popping bubbles.

Put at the bottom of a dessert glass 2 mL baking soda and 7.5 mL icing sugar. Pour apple cider on top and watch it froth and fizzle.

Nathan brings the biggest pumpkin he can carry from the patch. His mother needs it for her pumpkin pie.

The Thanksgiving feast

The settlers celebrated the harvest with a huge Thanksgiving dinner. The Christmas and Thanksgiving meals of the settlers were very similar. There were many courses of meats, vegetables, and desserts. The only difference was in the foods that were symbolic of special times of the year. The plum pudding was served only at Christmas. Pumpkin pie was usually served at the Thanksgiving table. The Christmas menu we put together can also be prepared as a Thanksgiving feast. Just substitute the pudding for the pie and serve the Hot Apple Cider Punch as your drink.

Pumpkin pie

375 mL	cooked pumpkin
175 mL	brown sugar
5 mL	cinnamon
3 mL	ginger
2 mL	salt
2	eggs, slightly beaten
375 mL	milk
120 mL	cream

Cook the filling in a double boiler until thick. Cool it slightly and pour into a baked pie shell.

Hot apple cider punch

4 L	apple cider
200 mL	sugar
2	lemons, studded with cloves
10 mL	whole cloves
3	cinnamon sticks

Heat cider, cloves, cinnamon, and sugar to boiling. Cover and simmer for a half hour. Strain and pour into punch bowl. Put studded lemons into punch.

The eldest daughter in the family returns to her parents' home with her husband and children for Thanksgiving dinner. Thanksgiving Day was a joyful time when families came together to give thanks for happiness and health.

In the early days, children were not allowed to sit at the table with the adults. As shown in the picture, they waited for their parents to pass them food. There are so many dishes at this Thanksgiving dinner, however, that the children are not likely to go hungry.

Christmas menu

Clam chowder

Salmon croquettes

Roast turkey   Oyster stuffing

Stuffed roasted chickens

Haunch of venison   Maple-glazed ham

Goose with fruit stuffing

Potatoes   Turnips   Squash   Onions

Stuffed tomatoes   Stewed celery with cream

Cranberry sauce   Baked apples

Plum pudding   Hard sauce

Mince pie   Apple crumb cake

Walnuts

Cheese   Fruit

Coffee

Christmas dinner, the biggest meal of the year

Christmas dinner was the biggest and best meal of the year. The settler's table was loaded with all kinds of food. Of course, not everyone could afford a sumptuous meal such as the one we are suggesting. Many settlers felt lucky even to have seen a turkey. However, many settlers saved their best food for the Christmas season. Menus, such as the one opposite, were not unusual. In fact, the list of foods on the opposite page was taken from a very old cookbook. We have changed some of the items to include recipes that can be found throughout the pages of this book. In each case we have tried to substitute the same type of food as suggested in the original menu. If you want to have a huge Christmas dinner, settler style, try some of these recipes. They can be found with the help of the index. Some of the recipes are on the next few pages.

Minced pie without meat

3	apples, pared, cored, and minced
750 g	fresh suet
1.5 kg	raisins
5 mL	mace
5 mL	cinnamon
5 mL	powdered cloves
1.5 kg	powdered sugar
2 mL	salt
	rind of 4 lemons
	juice of 2 lemons
250 mL	cranberry juice
250 mL	cooking sherry

Preheat oven to 225° C. Mix ingredients. Put into unbaked pie shell (see recipe p. 21). Cover with top crust. Slash crust with 6 steam holes. Bake in a hot oven (225° C) for 15 minutes. Reduce the heat to 180° C and bake until crust is golden brown.

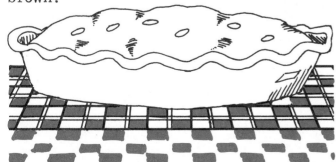

Cranberry-apple punch

3 L	cranberry juice
1 L	apple juice
100 mL	Raspberry Vinegar (see p. 19)
1 L	lemonade
300 mL	sugar
1	lemon

Heat cranberry juice and sugar to boiling, stirring constantly. When sugar has dissolved, take from heat and allow juice to cool. Mix in other ingredients and pour into punch bowl. Add ice. Float lemon slices on top as decoration.

Evelyn heats the cranberry-apple punch over the fire.

The glorious plum pudding parade

Children volunteered for the job of mixing the plum pudding ingredients.

There is no creature on earth who

The symbol of Christmas

The plum pudding was the symbol of Christmas for the settlers. No matter how little or how much the settlers had to eat for Christmas dinner, the pudding was always the main event. The tradition of the pudding can be traced back many hundreds of years in England. Christians used to fast before Christmas each year. The period of fasting was called *Advent*. During this time of fasting people ate a porridge called *frumenty*. This was later mixed with sausages called *hackin*. The mixture of the two resulted in the plum pudding. As years went by, more and more ingredients were added to the pudding. Most of the meat was replaced by fruit and nuts.

When people emigrate to a new country they often want to keep traditions that were dear to them in their old countries. When the British settlers came to the New World they wanted to celebrate Christmas in the old way. The plum pudding became more important to them than it ever had been. It was a way to hold on to past customs. The plum pudding made the settlers feel that they could follow the same lifestyle in their new homes as they had in the old. The pudding recalled the good times they shared with friends and relatives. It reminded them of the love they felt for each other. The Christmas pudding symbolized the miracle that is Christmas.

... can resist luscious plum pudding!

Ella ties her first plum pudding in a cloth. She will boil it now and share it with her friends at Christmas.

Plum pudding

250 mL	*light raisins*
250 mL	*dark raisins*
500 mL	*currants*
200 mL	*grated orange and lemon peel*
200 mL	*cooking sherry*
250 mL	*grated carrots*
500 mL	*suet, finely chopped*
1.5 L	*bread crumbs*
60 mL	*flour*
300 mL	*brown sugar*
2 mL	*mace*
2 mL	*nutmeg*
5 mL	*ginger*
8	*eggs, well beaten*

About 4 weeks before Christmas mix the first 4 ingredients together in a bowl. Pour cooking sherry over top of fruit. Let the fruit soak for about 1 week in the sherry. Stir the fruit often during the course of the week. Mix all of the other ingredients together with your fruit. Mix well. Tie the dough into a cloth firmly, but leave enough room for the mixture to swell. Boil it in the cloth for at least 5 hours. Do not let it stop boiling. Store the pudding at least 3 weeks in a cool, dry place to develop full flavor. On Christmas day, steam pudding 30–40 minutes. Serve with hard sauce (see p.43).

This cook spent more time decorating her peacock pie than she did cooking it. Peacock pie was a treat to taste and to look at.

The settlers roasted chickens, ducks, geese, turkeys, and even pheasants for their Christmas dinners. Turkeys and geese were the biggest Christmas favorites. We have found two good recipes, shown below. One is for turkey, and one is for goose. Try both.

The Christmas birds

Turkey with oyster stuffing

1	turkey, about 5 kg
1 L	bread crumbs, toasted until brown in the oven
120 mL	butter, taken from fridge and cut in bits
120 mL	chopped celery
120 mL	chopped onion
3 mL	savory
3 mL	thyme
500 mL	oysters
	salt to taste
	pepper to taste

Cook the celery and onion in butter in a frying pan until both are transparent. Do not brown. Chop each oyster into 4 pieces. Add oysters, herbs, and spices to the vegetables and continue cooking 3-4 minutes until oysters are firm.

Rub the turkey inside and out with salt and pepper. (Cook and chop the giblets and use them in the gravy.) Mix all of the ingredients and stuff into turkey. A small turkey will need to be cooked about 4 hours at 170° C.

Goose with fruit stuffing

1	large goose
500 mL	dried apple rings
500 mL	canned peach slices, without syrup
500 mL	raisins, rinsed in hot water
500 mL	canned apricots, without liquid
500 mL	pitted prunes, soaked overnight in cooking sherry
250 mL	dry bread crumbs
3 mL	ginger
3 mL	cinnamon
8	cloves
3 mL	nutmeg
1	egg

Preheat oven to 225° C. Salt and pepper goose on the inside and outside. Mix the fruit, bread crumbs, egg, and spices. Stuff goose and roast, covered, for 1 hour. Pour off fat, and reduce heat to 160° C. Add 250 mL water to pan and roast uncovered, basting with the fat drippings from time to time. Cover the goose with foil when skin is nicely browned. Baste often in the last hour with the syrup from the canned peaches and apricots.

The blessing of food

Be present at our table, Lord,
Be here and everywhere adored,
These mercies bless and grant that we
May feast in paradise with thee.

Glossary

alder a tree with rough bark and rounded leaves which grows in damp, cool areas

auger a tool used to drill holes

bacteria extremely small organisms which can produce disease or spoilage

barter to trade goods for something of equal value

baste to pour melted fat or other liquids over food as it roasts

bearings feelings or knowledge of direction a person has

bladder a bag-like part of the body which stores urine

chive a plant with grass-like leaves which are used for seasoning

chowder a thick soup made with fish or shellfish

colander a bowl with holes in the side and base, used for draining liquids from food

creosote an oil from coal tar used to preserve and disinfect food

croquette food minced, shaped into patties, coated, and fried

domesticate to tame; to raise something so it will be useful to people

elk a large North American deer

essence the concentrated liquid of a substance

export to sell and send goods to another country

ferment to cause the sugar in a liquid to turn into alcohol

frost line the depth to which frost penetrates the ground

game animals, birds or fish which people hunt

giblet the heart, liver, or gizzard of a fowl

ginger a plant root used as a spice

grate to shred

griddle a flat metal pan or surface used for cooking

grouse a plump brown or grey bird that was often hunted for food

harvest to gather or collect a ripened crop of grain, fruit or vegetables; the crop itself; the time or the season of such a gathering

haunch a cut of meat from the side, back and leg of an animal

hickory a tree with hard wood and edible nuts

hull the small leaves that grow by the stem of a fruit

husk the outer covering of certain fruits or seeds, especially corn; to remove a husk

impurity something that pollutes another substance

ingredient an item of food listed in a recipe

joint a large cut of meat used for roasting

knead to fold, press and stretch dough

ladle a long-handled spoon that can transfer a lot of liquid

loin a cut of meat from the side and back of an animal

mace a spice made from part of the covering of a nutmeg

mince to cut or chop into small pieces

mincemeat a mixture of chopped apples, raisins, spices, and sometimes meat, used as a pie filling

mutton the flesh or meat of a sheep

navy bean a white variety of the kidney bean

nutmeg the egg-shaped seed of a tropical tree used as a spice when ground

nutrition the process by which food is taken in and used by the body for growth and nourishment

pare to remove the outer skin of a fruit or vegetable with a knife or other sharp tool

quail a small, brown, plump bird with a short tail

resource a source of wealth or help

saltpeter a transparent white chemical used to pickle meat

sap the fluid that flows through a tree or plant, carrying food and other substances

savory a plant with leaves that are used for seasoning

seasoning a herb or spice added to food to give it more flavor

seedling a young plant grown from a seed

shortening a fat, such as lard or butter, used to make pastry light or flaky

sift to put through a sieve in order to separate into fine particles

simmer to boil gently

spile a device put into the side of a tree to draw off sap

staple a basic food or other product that is needed and used often

sterilize to clean germs and dirt from something

suet the hard, fatty tissue found around the kidneys of animals

tallow a substance made by boiling down fat, used in making candles

tradition a way of thinking or behaving which does not change for a great many years

venison the meat of a deer

whey the watery part of the milk left after curd has formed during the making of cheese

yeast used in bread-making; a substance which helps the loaf to rise

Index

Advertisements 70–1

Animals 10–3, 17, 24–5, 27, 32
  and maple syrup, 24–5; bagging, 17; hunting, 10–1, 27; raising domestic animals, 32; trapping, 12–3, 17, 27

Apples 52–4
  apple bee, 52–3; apple butter, 53; apple cider, 53; apple harvest, 52–3; apple sauce, 53–4.

Barter 5, 26, 29–30

Beans, baked with pork 25, 36–7

Bees 51–3

Berries See Fruits and Berries

Beverages 19, 24, 53, 83–4, 87
  apple cider, 53; cranberry apple punch, 87; hot apple cider punch, 84; maple beer, 24; maple wine, 24; minute champagne, 83; raspberry quencher, 19

Biscuits, Breads and Cakes 25, 27, 41, 43, 48, 55, 77, 82
  apple crumb cake, 55; bread pudding, 43; Irish soda bread, 82; Johnny Cake, 25, 48; milk toast, 43; old-fashioned flapjacks, 41, 43; thimble biscuits, 77; Welsh rabbit, 43

Blacksmith 57

Blessing 94

Bread-baking 38–42, 58–9. See also Biscuits, Breads and Cakes

Breakfast 48

Brine 66

Butter-making 44–6

Buttermilk 44–5

Buying food 69
Cheese 43, 47
  making cheese, 47; Welsh rabbit, 43
Chicken See Poultry
Christmas 4, 84, 86–93
Corn 27–9. See also Vegetable Recipes
Crops 4–5, 28, 30
  bartered for animals, 5; the planting of, 4–5, 28, 30
Desserts and Sweets 21, 24–5, 33, 43, 55, 76, 79–81, 83–4, 87, 91
  apple crumb cake, 55; apple snow, 55; baked apples, 55; blueberry pie, 21; bread pudding, 43; Dutch apple pudding, 83; easy banana ice cream, 79; freezer churn ice cream, 79; ginger drops, 76; maple sweeties, 24–5; minced pie without meat, 87; molasses taffy, 24, 81; plain taffy, 80; plum pudding, 91; pumpkin pie, 84; soft custard, 33
Dinner 49
Eggs 33, 67
  preserving, 67; use in cooking, 33. See also Egg Recipes
Egg Recipes 33, 82
  Scotch eggs, 82; soft custard, 33; stuffed eggs, 33
Fireplace 56–8, 60
  dangers of, 57–8; implements, 56–7; stoves as improvement on, 60. See also Ovens and Stoves
Fish 4, 6–9, 64
  broiling, 6–7; drying and smoking, 64; methods of catching, 4, 6–7; varieties, 6–9. See also Fish Recipes
Fish Recipes 7–9, 76, 83
  catch-of-the-day soup, 7; clam chowder, 9; German cod and potatoes, 83; salmon croquettes, 8; sardine sandwiches, 76; white sauce for fish, 8
Fruits and Berries 18–21, 52–3, 66–7
  apple harvest, 52–3; preserving, 20–1; varieties, 18–9.
Game See Animals
Goose See Poultry
Gravy and Sauce Recipes 8, 11, 35, 43
  everyday gravy, 35; hard sauce, 43; venison gravy, 11; white sauce for fish, 8
Grocery Stores 69–70
Homemaking 72–3
Hunting See Animals
Ice cream 78–9. See also Desserts and Sweets
Ice houses 66–7
Indians teach settlers 4–6, 26–8, 64
  how to cook and grow vegetables, 6, 26–8; how to make pemmican, 64; how to plant crops, 5; how to tap trees for sap, 23
International cookery 82–3
Jams 21, 43, 66
  how to make, 66; pumpkin marmalade, 43; strawberry jam, 21
Kitchens 58. See also Ovens and Stoves
Kitchen utensils 36–7, 57, 60, 62–3
  pots and pans, 36–7, 57, 60; gadgets, 62–3

Maple syrup See Sugar-maple tree. See also Animals
Meat 64–5
  made into pemmican, 64; pickling, smoking and potting, 65. See also Meat Recipes
Meat Recipes 11, 25, 36–7
  baked beans with pork, 25, 36–7; bubble and squeak, 37; Irish lamb stew, 37; venison roast, 11
Natural resources 5
Ovens and Stoves 4, 58–61
Pastry See Pies and Puddings
Pemmican 64
Pies and Puddings 21, 43, 48
  hasty pudding, 48; bread pudding, 43; pie crust, 21; plum pudding, 84, 88–91. See also Desserts and Sweets
Poultry 5, 16–7, 32
  crops bartered for, 5; raising, 32; varieties, 16–7. See also Poultry Recipes
Poultry Recipes 35, 93
  crispy fried chicken, 35; goose with fruit stuffing, 93; roast chicken with stuffing and gravy, 35; turkey with oyster stuffing, 93
Preserving 64–7, 70
  canning, 67, 70; pickling, smoking and potting, 64–7. See also Fruits and Berries
Rice 29
Root cellars 66–7
Salads 31, 82
  dandelion greens salad, 82; hot slaw, 31
Sauces See Gravy and Sauce Recipes
Servants, domestic 72–3
Smokehouse 65
Soups 9, 31, 83
  clam chowder, 9; French pea soup, 83; hearty potato soup, 31
Springhouses 67
Storing food 66–7
Stoves See Ovens and Stoves
Stuffings 35, 93
  fruit stuffing, 93; oyster stuffing, 93; poultry stuffing, 35
Sugar 22–26
Sugar-maple tree 22–6, 51
  maple sap, 22–6; maple sugar, 22–5; maple syrup, 22–6; molasses, 23–4; sugaring-off, 22–4, 51. See also Desserts and Sweets
Supper 49
Table manners 74–5
Taffy 80–1. See also Desserts and Sweets
Tea parties 76–7
Thanksgiving 4, 84–5
Trapping See Animals
Turkey See Poultry
Vegetables 27–8, 30. See also Vegetable Recipes
Vegetable Recipes 29, 31, 37, 82–3
  bubble and squeak, 37; corn stew, 29; dandelion greens salad, 82; hearty potato soup, 31; hot slaw, 31; stewed celery with cream, 31; stuffed tomatoes, 31; Ukrainian cabbage rolls, 83

Acknowledgements

Library of Congress, Dover Archives, Colonial Williamsburg, Scugog Shores Museum, Port Perry, Century Village, Lang, Upper Canada Village, Black Creek Pioneer Village, Metropolitan Toronto Library, Colborne Lodge, Toronto Historical Board, Gibson House, City of North York, Harper's Weekly, Bibliotheque National du Quebec, Canadian Illustrated News, Public Archives of Canada, Ontario Archives, Frank Leslie's Illustrated Magazine, the Osborne Collection of Early Children's Books, Toronto Public Library, the Buffalo and Erie County Public Library Rare Book Department, Jamestown, Chatterbox, Little Wide Awake, Harper's Round Table Magazine, Montgomery's Inn, Peterborough Postcard Company, John P. Robarts Research Library, Thomas Fisher Rare Book Library, William Blackwood and Sons.
789 BP Printed in Canada 09